To Betsy,
In appreciation for
sharing your beautiful journey
with me. Blessings in all
your journeys.

Embracing
the End-of-Life Journey

A beautiful story of learning to share the gifts of
compassion, spiritual connection and peace

Wendy Jordan

Wendy Jordan

BALBOA
PRESS
A DIVISION OF HAY HOUSE

Balboa Press books may be ordered through booksellers or by contacting:

Balboa Press
A Division of Hay House
1663 Liberty Drive
Bloomington, IN 47403
www.balboapress.com
1 (877) 407-4847

Printed in the United States of America.

ISBN: 978-1-4525-9306-7 (sc)
ISBN: 978-1-4525-9307-4 (hc)
ISBN: 978-1-4525-9308-1 (e)

Library of Congress Control Number: 2014903268

Balboa Press rev. date: 03/27/2014

This book is dedicated
with love
to my mother Ruth and my daughter Sarah

Contents

~ ~

Introduction

I have been unbelievably blessed to be able to facilitate "end-of-life" spiritual treatments. This was not something I ever thought I would be doing for other people when I first became aware of energy healing and studied the Japanese hands-on healing art called Reiki. I simply wanted to learn more about holistic healing techniques and open my own consciousness to being more "aware and connected" to loved ones as they approached the end of their lives. It was something I needed to do for *me,* after my own father died.

But apparently I was not alone in my longings. Many people feel the need to do something more for their dying loved ones… something beyond, and in addition to, traditional hospice or clergy visits. As the physical body quiets, tires and changes, and more time is spent sleeping or unconscious, this is the time to connect with loved ones on a soul level. This is a time to embrace each other, not only in the physical, but in some other way… a way that feels timeless and complete.

Knowing that your loved ones are experiencing feelings of connection to you is extremely comforting, even in an unconscious state. Reiki treatments performed with these intentions can have profoundly comforting and healing results.

Having never had a near death experience, I cannot know exactly what the Reiki energy does on that higher spiritual plane. Each situation feels different, so I don't have an exact plan of what I will do. I just know that as each treatment evolves, I usually feel that at a certain point, I am being spiritually guided and no two treatments are ever alike. I believe that in the quiet moments, with the Universal Life Force Energy flowing through me, the words I speak and the actions I take with family members are divinely inspired. I am sometimes moved to tears myself as I experience, with the family, the most amazing connections, emotions, revelations and moments of complete peace. I am always grateful and very humbled by the experience.

I also am aware that sometimes the true reason I am called to do an end-of-life, spiritual treatment is a desperate hope that there will be a miraculous physical healing. Often, families in denial hope that their loved one will awaken from a coma or suddenly go into a complete remission from a disease. Others are hoping their loved ones will say some last coherent words to be remembered after years of separation due to Alzheimer's or dementia.

When I become aware of this, I explain that although we can always pray for a miracle, this particular type of healing is not about suddenly curing a disease or waking up free of illness. Reiki healing at the time near death is about helping the process of finishing ones physical experience on earth, and moving back to the spiritual — a birthing, so to speak. It's about helping the family to understand that non-verbal communication can be achieved through what is called journeying. And through this journeying process, the awareness of the spiritual connection to their loved ones is strengthened and will always remain.

The experiences in this book span a 12-year period. Since I didn't plan to write about them, I didn't keep notes and I never record sessions. However, eventually I began to feel that the experiences I've had might be helpful for others who are helping their sick or elderly family members, hospice workers, or anyone who is interested in considering how they would like to experience their end-of-life journey.

All of these chapters are about real people and real experiences, but I chose not to use any real names. Some of the details may not be exact because when I am doing this work the Reiki energy relaxes me into a place where my mind quiets all thoughts, allowing for spiritual guidance to come through. Sometimes after the sessions I don't always remember all the details. In some cases I have contacted the families to confirm my memories or get their perspective on how our sessions together affected the experience when death finally occurred.

I hope that I have represented these beautiful people with dignity and admiration. Those who have passed and those who sat with me as we Reiki-journeyed into spirit together have been my most valuable teachers and I will be forever grateful.

1

Mrs. O'Reilly's Garden

It was a perfect day for a drive... warm breezes, cloudless blue skies, the forest preserves filling the air with moist, green smells and summer flowers in full bloom. I was driving north through one of the loveliest neighborhoods in the northern suburbs of Chicago. Mature trees lined the road and the sunlight flickered through the leaves.

I often drove through these winding streets to admire the beautiful mansions with their extravagant gardens, lush landscaping and magnificent architecture. Sometimes, I'd turn and drive eastward towards Lake Michigan to gaze out at the miles of shoreline and soak in the serenity of the swaying blue water. Often I'd stop, take off my shoes and feel the warm sand, breathe in the moisture and get lost in thought as I peered out into the horizon.

But on this day there was no time to stop. I had an appointment to facilitate a spiritual healing session in a private home, and so I was taking this slow, beautiful route to calm myself and feel connected to nature and spirit as I approached an experience that I knew would be different from any I'd had before.

I had become a practitioner of the hands-on energy healing modality called Reiki. Many believe that Reiki is the oldest form of energy healing, and was re-discovered and reintroduced in the 1920s, by a Japanese man named Mikao Usui. I had taken all the classes to become a Reiki Master and teacher. This meant several years of studying the different levels of hands-on energy healing, along with some other courses in healing and spirituality, starting my own practice to do private sessions, lecturing around the Chicago area to raise awareness of complementary and holistic healing techniques, and eventually teaching Reiki to others. I had also spent time "practicing" Reiki by volunteering to work in hospice.

Previously, hospice had sent me to nursing homes, hospitals and some private homes. But today was going to be different. I could feel it. And the main reason was because I was not going on a visit assigned by hospice. I had been called directly by a family that was looking for an energy healer to be with their mother in her final weeks of life, perhaps providing some spiritual insights as well as physical comfort. This was going to be much more than a Reiki session, and I was preparing myself.

Mrs. O'Reilly had round-the-clock nursing care, and a personal assistant who had been with her for many years. She was in her eighties and her husband was in his nineties. They had several grown children and many grandchildren. Mrs. O'Reilly was now in her bed in a guest bedroom, not the bedroom she had shared with her husband for so many years. As her illness progressed, her daughter Alice, who now lived in New Orleans, came to help her through her final days.

Alice convinced her family that although hospice was coming in once a week, they needed someone to add a different level of comfort and healing for their mother. She wasn't ready for a priest, and had said she didn't really want anyone "religious" coming to visit. She had asked her holistic practitioner if he knew anyone who could do some kind of "spiritual healing session" with her mother. He referred me.

I was prepared. I had packed calming essential oils, an assortment of crystals, beautiful flute and harp music, and a candle. I had meditated and called on my guides and the angels to be with me. But as I was getting close to the house, I found myself a little anxious, so I turned on the radio, turned off the air conditioning and rolled down the window to feel the warm summer air in my face. Solsbury Hill, a song by Peter Gabriel was playing. I've always loved that song — it has such a joyful and spiritual feeling to it, although I never really knew all the words.

> *"Climbing up on Solsbury Hill*
> *I could see the city lights*
> *Wind was blowing time stood still*
> *Eagle flew out of the night..."*

Hawks and eagles have always had a very mystical meaning for me, they seem to appear at very significant times. Could this also be one of them? I started to pay even more attention to the song lyrics as I hummed along with the music. I was relaxed and peaceful.

But suddenly, I was hearing the song in a different way and it seemed to be talking to me about death. Could that be? I listened more closely to the lyrics.

> *"...My heart going boom boom boom.*
> *'Son,' he said, 'grab your things,*
> *I've come to take you home."*

Suddenly *my* heart pounded too! "Oh my God, it's a sign." I thought to myself. And I was consumed with the thought that this was Spirit's way of telling me that Mrs. O'Reilly would die while I was there with her. Perhaps this was *her* day to "go home!"

Although I had been trained in hospice, spent six months with one patient, a few weeks each with several others, and then visited with some friends' parents after strokes and heart attacks, I had never witnessed the moment of death. Not even after being at my own father's bedside for weeks, did I share that moment when he drew his last breath and his spirit left his body. I had always been sad that I didn't witness that special moment with him. Now I wondered if it was my time to be with and help "birth" someone from this physical realm back to spirit.

Was I prepared? Why was I so nervous when I had always felt this was part of my path? I had to gather myself and found myself pleading to my spirit helpers, the angels, the Almighty... anyone who was listening.

"I really want to be there for comfort and healing, but do you *really* think I'm ready for this?" I asked out loud. "Are you sure I can handle this properly?" We wouldn't be in the hospital. I didn't have a caseworker to ask if I had any questions. And I didn't know this family at all. Oh, how I hoped this would just be a simple, calming, uneventful Reiki treatment!

Then I relaxed. Maybe I *was* ready. Maybe I needed to let myself be led by Spirit and just do what I had learned to do and trust that I had been brought to this family at the right time for the right reason. I took a deep breath and headed to the door.

I found myself at the double doors of an exquisite home where I was greeted by a man in his sixties. Joseph was the dying woman's son. He was trying to look cheerful but I could see sadness all around him. We walked up a beautiful open staircase to the second floor, and I was brought in to Mrs. O'Reilly's bedroom.

It was beautifully decorated in yellows and white and was very cheerful. There were fresh flowers and pictures of loved ones on her dresser, with a comfortable wing chair at the bedside. A balcony door and many windows all trimmed in lace, gave a stunning view of the yard below. Her electric bed, or "comfort bed" as I like to call it, was in the center of the room so that medical equipment could easily reach her.

I spoke with Joseph as I prepared... learning a little about the family and his mother's condition. Mrs. O'Reilly was awake. She was a lovely woman who extended her hand when I was introduced. I asked if she wanted to hear some soft music and explained that I would be doing energy work to help her feel calm and alleviate any pain she might be feeling.

I always begin my work with a silent prayer, and then have a particular way of scanning the body to get information about what is going on and where I need to work. I also use the Reiki symbols to put love and emotional healing into her auric field and do some balancing of the energy system before I sit down and start sending the healing energy to the body. When I was seated at her head, I began doing a traditional Reiki treatment while she asked a few questions and we talked.

After about twenty minutes, I noticed that her son was lingering near the door and it seemed as if he really wanted to come in. I asked if he would like to sit with us, and I had him sit next to his mother and invited him to hold her hand.

Mrs. O'Reilly had closed her eyes and dozed off into what I call a Reiki slumber... a sleep that remains very close to consciousness, so that I can still feel reaction to what I am doing. I had planned on continuing my "full body treatment" with some explanation and conversation with Joseph along the way.

Then suddenly everything changed. Instead of "feeling" the energy of Mrs. O'Reilly, all I could feel was the deep sadness in Joseph and I knew he wanted so much to "connect" with his mother. I knew that feeling. I had felt that very thing at my own father's bedside. During my father's final days, it was my biggest frustration that I was losing my ability to connect with and really *be* there with my dad.

I remember putting the Reiki "love" symbol in the air between Joseph and his mother and wishing I had the right words to comfort him. And that's when the lesson came. The inspiration. A gift.

The energy in the room shifted, I became very still and quiet. I allowed the guidance to come through and I heard myself say, "Joseph, would you like to spend a little time connecting with your mother… being able to say to her exactly what's in your heart without having to speak any words?"

Did I really say that? Why? How? What was I going to do?

I heard him say, "Yes, I'd really like that" and he looked at me with moist eyes. I then relaxed back into one of the most beautiful spiritual journeys I've ever taken. A Reiki journey into the timeless place of the heart where we can connect with, feel and communicate with our loved ones… anytime, anywhere, always. And I listened to myself speak the words that were being put there for me say. They were coming not from my head, but directly from my heart.

Mrs. O'Reilly was still asleep so I guided Joseph through the journey. "I want you to think of the most comforting, wonderful, nurturing and safe place that your mother would like to be. Somewhere that she could sit and enjoy being with you and others she loves." I told him it could be a real place or imagined. Someplace they've been together, or somewhere she always wanted to go.

I knew that by allowing their minds and spirits to flow out of the room and go somewhere else that was created energetically rather than physically, they would begin a communication through thought, instead of words. It's a meditation technique used often to connect with our guides or do other healing work. But I'd never used the technique in this way before.

He knew where to go right away. He told me that she loved the big gardens right down below her bedroom window. She loved to sit there alone or with family, do some gardening or reading or just quietly enjoying a cup of tea. She hadn't been able to get up to look down at the garden for a while.

We began. Although Mrs. O'Reilly was asleep, I spoke to both of them and asked them to visualize being in the garden, sitting next to each other. I told them to really look around and see the beauty, feel the warm air, notice the birds, flowers or any other comforting thing that might be there in their perfect garden. And then I told them to feel each other's energy. To feel the warmth around each other and to try to settle into just "being" with each other without any words or thoughts.

After a few minutes, I knew that Joseph really wanted to say something to his mother. I invited him to talk to her, to say whatever he needed to, or wanted to. I told him to ask her questions, to express his feelings, and then to wait for her response. But I asked him to do this without any words, to just visualize or imagine all these things happening in the garden.

I sat. It was silent. I put the Reiki symbol for emotional healing over them and then used the symbol for compassionate love. I sat some more.

And then the most beautiful thing happened. My heart opened and *I* could feel what *they* were feeling. It wanted to burst it was so full of love. I could feel them communicating. I realized my eyes had been closed and when I opened them I saw Joseph crying, but with a beautiful smile on his face. And his mother was smiling too.

"That's your heart connection," I said. "That's the connection that has always been there and will never be lost." I allowed them more time to silently communicate.

And then I spoke words that seemed to have come from somewhere else than my own mind... words that I will never forget. "You can come to the garden to talk to your mother whenever you need to. You can come back tomorrow, you can come back when she's not conscious, and you can come back here in two months, or in two years... forever."

I was being shown how a spiritual connection could be maintained though intention, with or without the physical body. Could it really be that after someone dies, you can still communicate by focusing thoughts and intention through guided meditation? And was it the presence of Reiki energy that helped facilitate it? I knew I still had much to learn.

I stayed quiet after that. I still felt the Reiki energy flowing out of my hands into her physical body. But Spiritual healing was also taking place, a much more profound healing.

This was also the beginning of a new way for me to practice my energy healing. I realized that the experience I had just witnessed was the experience I wished I had had with my own father. Maybe now, I could help others to avoid the frustrating feeling of losing the connection with someone as they journey on to the next realm after their death.

After awhile Joseph left the room and I finished my treatment. Mrs. O'Reilly awoke and I told her that Joseph had been there for some of the treatment. She said she knew and very lightheartedly questioned why it is always so hard for sons to tell their mothers how they feel. She also told me that she had already known everything he felt he needed to say.

I couldn't believe it. She had experienced "the Garden" with her son. And yet I believe at that point that the biggest healing happened for Joseph.

When I left her room Joseph was waiting for me and he looked so much more vibrant and happy. He told me that at first he felt like he was saying goodbye, and then he realized he was saying hello to his mother in a new way. He was allowing himself to now know his mother through a heart connection, not the physical human way of communicating that they had known for over sixty years. So he didn't say goodbye. He just said he loved her.

As I was leaving, Joseph and his sister Alice asked if I would return in a few days when their other sister, Susan, would be arriving from Italy. Susan hadn't seen her mother for quite a few years and was feeling guilty about having moved her family out of the country. I said I would.

Once I was back in my car I knew that something very special had happened. Could it be repeated? I knew I didn't need to think about or plan my next session. My guidance would be there for me, giving me the next lesson and using me as a facilitator for more healing. So although I could identify with Peter Gabriel's words, "I did not believe the information, I just had to trust imagination, my heart going boom boom boom…" I was *very* grateful that it wasn't Mrs. O'Reilly's time to "go home." I had a lot more to learn.

2

Return to the Garden

I returned to the O'Reilly house several days later. I began her treatment the same way I usually do, with some silent Reiki prayer, some energy balancing and aligning, and then flowing the energy for fifteen or twenty minutes, just to get Mrs. O'Reilly to relax and to let go of any stresses or pains in her body. This also gave me time to talk with Mrs. O'Reilly for a while. She was so lovely as she gave me little insights into her life. By now I knew they were a very well known family that had created a legacy in business as well as a family fortune. I was honored to be working with them at this time, and very much aware that their privacy must always be protected.

As always, we discussed any physical discomfort she might be having and then I let her relax into the treatment. After about twenty minutes, I asked if her daughter would like to join us, knowing that Susan really wanted to have some healing time with her mother.

Susan entered the room. She was nervous. This was a whole different energy. But I decided not to ask any questions about her apprehensions, and just let her join in the treatment.

I explained to her that Joseph thought the garden was a good place to visualize together with Mrs. O'Reilly. She agreed. Mrs. O'Reilly was now asleep. Susan sat and held her mother's hand as I began to guide them through the garden path to seats on a bench. I began my explanation of how she could talk to her mother, in thought only, without speaking words… but before I could say more, Susan began to sob and put her head on her mother's hand. I didn't say anything further. I closed my eyes and continued to send healing energy to both Susan and Mrs. O'Reilly.

Before long, Susan became calm. Finally, she got up, thanked me and left the room. I didn't have the same connection or awareness as I had with Joseph, so I wondered what had happened. I would find out later.

After Susan left the room, Mrs. O'Reilly woke. She was so glad that Susan had spent some time with her. She told me that Susan lived in Italy and she hadn't visited with the grandchildren for a while. Then she confided in me that Susan had felt badly because she wasn't living in the country and thought Mrs. O'Reilly was angry that they were living abroad. Susan also was feeling guilty that she hadn't been around to help with her mother's needs as her health deteriorated. Mrs. O'Reilly was able to communicate with her daughter that she was never angry at her choice of living in Italy… that on the contrary, she was glad that her daughter was happy and providing a wonderful life for her grandchildren. She did miss her grandchildren, but had accepted the situation. Now, she was glad they were all there and was very anxious to see them. She had given her daughter the forgiveness she was seeking, but ultimately, she communicated to Susan that there was nothing to forgive.

Then, Mrs. O'Reilly surprised me again. Instead of asking to see the grandchildren, she asked if she could do some connection with her personal secretary, Dorothy.

Dorothy had been with her for many years and currently lived in the house. I could tell that Dorothy was her closest confidant and friend. I was so thrilled that Mrs. O'Reilly was totally aware of the connection and closure that was happening, and that she wanted to journey with her dear friend, for some gratitude and closure. So we brought Dorothy in and I watched as, woman-to-woman, employee-to-boss, and friend-to-friend, Mrs. O'Reilly and her assistant Dorothy made another beautiful heart connection. This time words were spoken, but also, there was a quiet time of just being together. Mrs. O'Reilly stayed conscious as the two journeyed into the garden. I don't know what was said, but I feel that there was a lot of love and gratitude being shared.

I continued to visit twice a week and wondered why I had never met Mrs. O'Reilly's husband. One day I got my answer. It turned out that Mr. O'Reilly thought this was a bunch of hogwash! He would never have allowed some "woo woo" spiritual healer or Reiki Master to come visit his wife. So his children were sneaking me in!

"Hmmmm." As much as I was enjoying the times with the family... this didn't seem right to me. Alice told me that "soon" they would tell their father.

My appointments with Mrs. O'Reilly were being scheduled when her husband was out playing his morning golf game. They knew that he'd be gone for several hours, so I'd have plenty of time to set up, do my Reiki, visit a bit and then leave.

However, one day it rained unexpectedly and right in the middle of a session, Alice burst in and said I had to go. They blew out the candle and unplugged my CD player, while I quickly ended the session. I was then escorted to the back staircase! Wow, what a strange feeling *that* was. I was leaving through the back as their father was entering through the front.

13

I have no idea how they explained the car in the driveway or the smell of incense!

My visits were a little more spread out after that, and a few weeks later I was leaving to teach a class in New Mexico. I wondered if I'd ever see them again. My answer came when I returned home.

There was a lovely message from Alice, thanking me for all I did for the family and explaining that her mother had died while I was away. And then I heard the most wonderful news.

The children had told their father that I had been coming to visit. They told him about the garden and how they all would hold hands with their mother to spiritually connect and journey with her. Alice wrote that when her mother finally died, the whole family, including Mr. O'Reilly, Dorothy and the grandchildren, were gathered around her... all holding hands. I don't know how those final moments were spent together, but I do know that they were surrounded by spirit and ready to experience a peaceful journey... together.

> *"Wind was blowing time stood still*
> *Eagle flew out of the night..."*

Solsbury Hill, lyrics by Peter Gabriel

3

Angela Goes to Disneyland

My next experience of helping family members connect to their dying loved one was very different, because it was a younger member of the family who was terminally ill. There's an unnatural feeling when a family has to face the death of one of the younger members, a different kind of sadness. In this case, Angela was the middle child, in her early fifties.

Her older sister Rebecca was a student of mine. She just finished taking the second level of Reiki classes and was using meditation and energy to comfort her sister who was dying of cancer. Angela was at home, living in the family room where they had put her comfort bed, instead of the bedroom. Relatives were stopping by to visit and family members were with her round the clock. Being in the family room, just off the kitchen made visiting Angela feel very social and kept her connected to the outside world. It also allowed her father and siblings to be attentive to Angela while she readied herself for her journey into death.

On the day I came to visit, I again sat in my car for a few minutes and said some prayers and centered myself. I had the passing thought that I couldn't believe I was doing this. I had never expected that Reiki would lead me to be working with

15

people at the time of their death. Always squeamish around tubes, needles and blood, I pondered my new role as someone who walked into lives of total strangers at one of the most significant times of their lives. I took a deep breath and entered the home.

I could see Angela sitting up in her bed, but I asked Rebecca if I could first go to the washroom. I needed another minute. I decided to do my little ritual of "getting my Reiki energy flowing" while in the bathroom. As I closed my eyes and began, I saw the most beautiful, vibrant color purple fill my eyes. I had seen that exact purple color before... once during meditations in Sedona during my Reiki Master training, and once again on vacation on a beach in Tortola while I did an open-eyed meditation looking out at the ocean. I believed it was more than just colors and I now know it's the healing energy that is with me when I work. It was, and still is, beautiful and extremely comforting to me.

I was brought over to Angela and was delighted. Her eyes were smiling, and she welcomed me. She showed no signs of what she might be physically experiencing, and had no complaints. She had already experienced Reiki with her sister and was now anxious to get started with me. Again I used some of the essential oils that I find helpful in bringing in a sense of peace. And we put on some of my favorite spiritual music.

I started my session sitting by her head, while her sister sat and did energy work at her feet. When two people do energy work together, the vibration and warmth of the healing energy becomes even more powerful and the relaxation is profound. Eventually we decided to journey. And that's when I realized how diverse and surprising this type of experience could be.

Some other family members joined us, sitting next to Angela's bed. I was starting to go inward to listen to guidance as to how to proceed. I softly cradled Angela's head in my hands and asked her to relax and allow herself to begin to drift off. I told her I would like her to imagine herself floating out of her bed and going to a place that felt comforting, nurturing, healing and safe. It could be real or imagined, inside or out and she could bring anything into the environment that she would like. I told her that this would be a place where she could always go to connect with her loved ones, where they could send messages, communicate or just *be* together.

Often when people relax and allow themselves to drift off to somewhere else, they go someplace out in nature… a beach, the ocean, a clearing in the forest. As they journey I get a sense of the colors of where they are… blues and greens being very common. The gold of the sand or the sun sometimes becomes the strongest color. And occasionally people go into familiar, comforting places from their past, like their grandmother's living room or their childhood bedroom.

Angela's place was different. I was surprised to "intuitively see" a lot of pink and purple. I tried to see more of "where she was," because I was having trouble connecting with the concept of a pink place out in nature. Then, I actually started seeing visions… a new experience for me. There were peaks or spires or towers or something tall. I still couldn't figure it out, and Angela was obviously enjoying *being* wherever she was. Finally I had to ask, "Where are you?"

"I'm in the castle" she replied.

"The castle?" I asked. "What castle?"

"It's my favorite place, I love Disneyland and Disney World… I'm in the Disney Castle." And I swear, suddenly I saw the fireworks and colored lights just like they used to look on the *Wonderful World of Disney* TV show!

How beautifully unexpected! And how wondrously easy and fun it was for Angela to imagine herself in her favorite place. Rebecca, on the other hand, wasn't surprised at all... they all loved Disneyland and fantasy... her sister had chosen the perfect place! They were both smiling and the energy of the room became light and fun and magical.

I asked her to create a comfortable place to sit or lie down within the castle, expecting some pillows, couches or a luxurious bed. And I told her to imagine comfortable places for her visitors to sit as well.

I couldn't "see" anything. I struggled to be with the feeling she had inside the castle. I looked for the images in my head, but only seemed to get a feeling of a darkened room, almost like a large conference room. It didn't seem to fit the beautiful, pinks and purples. Finally I asked her if she was doing what I asked... had she created an environment to visit with her loved ones inside the castle?

Of course she had! But I still couldn't connect with what she had created, so I finally asked her what was in the room. She had created an entire "Knights of the Roundtable" type of room, with a big wooden table and large carved chairs with velvet cushions all around. Angela put herself at the head of the table... the "Queen Bee" so to speak. I'm sure her chair was more like a massive throne! Ahhh, now it made sense. I told her to imagine all her family members sitting in the castle with her. And as they held hands at her bedside, they journeyed with her in her castle.

What an amazing lesson for me, a lesson that spirit often reminds me of... Angela was having fun. Here was a woman facing her death and yet she was able to feel childlike creative and fun. What a blessing that she was able to find humor during a time of pain. Using our imaginations is one of the most healing and comforting techniques for relaxation and enjoyment. And what a joy it was to journey to the castle with Angela time and time again.

Most times that I came to the house, Angela's father was sitting by himself in the kitchen. He wasn't being a part of our sessions. My gut feeling was that he was feeling left out, as the women would hold hands, relax, speak softly and journey together. So one day I asked him if he'd like to join us. I did my opening prayers, and Rebecca and I sent Reiki energy to Angela's body, and their father sat at her side holding her hand. Despite Angela's enthusiasm for journeying back to the castle, I remember feeling her father's sadness. In this instance, even though I could feel a strong connection going on, and an awareness of lots of emotion, I had no sense of their communications. And that was ok. I don't know if he ever felt that he was "in the castle" although I'm sure Angela put him there! What mattered was that he was now closer to his daughter, holding her hand, being part of her journey. He no longer stayed in the kitchen while we gathered by her bed. He joined in.

It can be frustrating to be doing this kind of work and not be sure of what is happening... but let me assure you something wonderful *is* happening. Whether it is a moment of breaking through the bonds of fear, or sending loving thoughts to each other without using words, a spiritually guided healing *is* taking place. Those of us who are the facilitators are not always included. Our ego can get in the way or *their* spiritual messages are not meant for *us*. At those times, quiet your mind, try to "feel" with your heart and let spirit guide the session.

Eventually Angela and Rebecca were so good at journeying that they didn't need me. Angela loved to go to her castle and bring her family and friends with her. Rebecca told me later, that Angela used to get so tired of being in the bed, that she would ask to get helped into the bathroom, and then stay in there for long a time.

"People, people of the castle, come in and play with me!" Angela would shout from the bathroom. Rebecca still laughs when she thinks of how they would all pretend to be up in the beautiful pink castle in the sky that Rebecca had created. Not exactly how I had envisioned a spiritual journey, for sure. But fun, playful and indeed a healing form of connection that lasted well beyond Angela's death.

When I spoke to Rebecca some time after Angela died, I asked if everyone was with her at the time of her passing. I wondered if they were all able to gather in the castle together. Rebecca told me that even though Angela was in a very weak state and mentally ready to move on, she continued to get so excited when people were around that she wouldn't allow herself to relax enough to let go, finally releasing from her physical body. Angela's hospice worker suggested that everyone leave the house and leave Angela alone.

One evening they held a little party in the house for Angela. And, sure enough after they all left, when it was quiet and peaceful and only her husband and son were with her asleep on couches near her bed, Angela, with no one there to play with, finally let her spirit release from her body. My guess is that she headed straight for her castle.

> *"A dream is a wish your heart makes*
> *When you're fast asleep*
> *In dreams you lose your heartaches*
> *Whatever you wish for, you keep."*

A Dream is a Wish Your Heart Makes,
lyrics by Mack David, *Al Hoffman*
and Jerry Livingston

4
My Goodbye Gift

I had a best friend growing up. She was one of those friends who was more like a sibling. We did everything together all week long and on weekends we loved to have sleepovers. I came from a very small family, and Katie came from a large family. I loved staying at her house because she had three brothers and a sister and it was loud, busy and fun, unlike my house, which was usually pretty quiet. My parents were professional musicians so they were rarely home on Friday or Saturday nights. So rather than being alone, I preferred to go to the Cavelli house, where we had fun playing board games and puzzles, watching favorite Saturday night TV shows, or watching a TV movie. Katie's mom made the best pan-popped popcorn ever, and Katie's dad never tired of playing games with us kids.

Katie's father was one of those "fascinating" people that seemed to know how to fix everything, loved to read, preferred his bicycle to a car, and found it easy to welcome me into his already large family. He never tired of me hanging around acting like I totally belonged there. And I really did feel like I had a second family.

After college, Katie's siblings moved to different parts of the country, but when they all came back to celebrate the Cavelli's

50th wedding anniversary, I was there, included as part of the family. Eventually, Katie moved to California with her husband and children, but I'd still see the Cavelli family when she would come in for holidays. They all remained very special to me.

I remember my sadness on the afternoon when the call came from Katie telling me that her father had had a stroke. It was pretty severe and he wasn't expected to recover. She had just arrived in Chicago and the family was in the process of rounding up all the sisters and brothers from all over the country. Her mother was pretty much in shock, so Katie was very concerned for her, too. Her father remained in a coma.

Katie asked me to call her in the morning so I could set up a time to come visit them at the hospital. I knew I'd like to do some energy healing treatment on Mr. Cavelli, but I also knew the rest of the family would be there, very much in need of some calming and support.

I wasn't about to wait for "tomorrow." I hung up the phone, got in my car, and arrived at the hospital about twenty minutes later. Katie looked at me with a big smile and said, "What took you so long?'

I hugged my dear friend, and her very upset mother. Several of the other siblings were already there sitting in different parts of the room. The feeling of "we're just waiting and don't really know what else to do" was in the air.

Now I've never been particularly comfortable in hospitals, and I had never been to the bedside of one of my friends' parents. So I wondered, what should I do — be a visitor or an energy worker? Would my Reiki treatment be welcomed? It seemed too soon to try to get the family to journey. So I took a deep breath and allowed Spirit to guide me. I sat down next to Mr. Cavelli. I took his hand and found myself talking to him despite his unconscious state.

"Hi Mr. Cavelli, it's Wendy." I put my hand on his head and stroked his hair. I held his hand. I can't remember what else I said but I then looked at Katie and asked if it would be ok if I did a little healing work on him.

"Of course" she said, "we knew you would."

I told Mr. Cavelli (silently) that I was going to do energy work on him to send healing and balancing into his body. I took my place at his head, silently prayed and asked spirit to guide me. Then I gently cradled his head. Within minutes, the room settled, a peaceful vibration came over us. I knew everyone was feeling the vibration when Mrs. Cavelli settled back in her chair and said, "I don't understand what you're doing, but it sure feels relaxing." Within a few minutes *she* was sleeping in her chair.

The Cavelli's had been married for over sixty years and knew each other like they knew themselves. It didn't seem like they needed to journey to stay connected, they just needed to *be* together. And being together with all of their children was creating the perfect circumstances for Mr. Cavelli to feel at peace. Perhaps the individual family members may have benefited from journeying with their father, but at the time, providing a peaceful, relaxing environment in the midst of this sad situation was more important. The comfort would come in knowing that something beyond medical assistance was being provided for their father.

So although I decided not to do any kind of verbal meditation or journey with the family, I did do some journeying of my own. Mr. Cavelli was unconscious as I began to send healing energy into his body. I was very aware that this might be my final time with the other father that I had spent so much of my youth with. So I sent love. From my hands and from my heart I sent love. And with my thoughts, I sent gratitude and more love and pretty soon I felt like we were flying! No it wasn't flying, it was like riding a bike… something we all did together for years. Mr. Cavelli on his trusty old bicycle, and Katie and I rode a tandem bicycle next to him. I hadn't said a word to him verbally, but through my Reiki, I had quietly done my own journeying. I created the "journey place" and I felt him joining me there. I felt his joy and I was able to thank him for being like a father to me. I also used some energy techniques to connect his heart (the love energy center) to his crown chakra (the spiritual energy center) and then to expand his connection with spirit. This helps ease the process of letting go of our physical body and earthly connections, while the soul is moving back into the spiritual world. When I left, I felt I had truly been able to say goodbye to my dear friend that I had known since childhood. And I felt complete in my goodbye, knowing that I would not be there when he finally passed.

As I drove home, I felt wonderfully uplifted. Again, I had experienced turning to spiritual guidance and getting in the "zone" of doing Reiki. And I was amazed at how I became a person I almost didn't recognize at those times. I didn't like hospitals. I used to faint at blood and needles. I was uncomfortable and never knew what to say when people were sick, much less dying. And yet, there I was, able to easily come to the bedside of a friend and not fall apart or feel uncomfortable. This was the gift of living though the heart and turning myself over to higher guidance. Once again, the lesson of helping another person journey back to spirit became clearer… a lesson that started when my own father was dying and I felt helpless in assisting him. I now realized that although I was learning Reiki as a technique to share with other people, this was really becoming MY healing journey. The feeling of completion that I wasn't able to experience with my own father,

I was able to do with the man who had been like my second father for many years.

So how did I ever get to this place of higher understanding? How did this journey begin?

> *"You just call out my name,*
> *and you know wherever I am,*
> *I'll come running, to see you again*
> *Winter, spring, summer or fall,*
> *all you have to do is call*
> *And I'll be there, yeah,*
> *you've got a friend"*

You've Got a Friend, lyrics by Carol King

5

My Personal Experience with Death

I didn't know very much about death. Until you are faced with death, it's a scene in a movie, a headline in the newspaper or something that happens to other people. Sometimes I thought about it, but, like most children, I didn't put much attention on it.

Until I was in my twenties, the only experiences I'd had with death were surprising and sudden. The first death of someone I knew happened when some of my neighbors were in a terrible car accident. Suddenly, a mother and her three sons, which included a little boy in my 3rd grade class who I rode the bus with, and laughed and played with... weren't there anymore. Gone. I would never see them again. It was a strange concept to understand and I was very sad.

Besides an announcement on the school intercom system, followed by some nice words and a prayer, that was it! One day I had a friend, the next day he was gone. There weren't any group conversations, or a service for children to attend. It was just over. There was now a small hole in my heart that I had no idea how to fill.

The next year President Kennedy was assassinated! Shocking. Frightening. Sad. We collectively watched television together, witnessing other people's grief and all the collective fear and disorientation that came about at that time. Again, there wasn't a conversation about death and dying, how to deal with it, or what happens next. Instead, death was a terribly sudden event, a crime, an accident, and something that put us all in shock.

For the next few years, we watched clips of the Viet Nam War come into our living rooms every evening, giving us body counts, and at the same time desensitizing us to death. My generation collectively observed political leaders being assassinated, rock stars dying from drug overdoses and people in other countries that died en masse from natural disasters or wars. Most of the deaths in my world were quick, with no time for preparation.

I was also part of a generation very different from our parents, the "baby boomers." And the way I reacted to all this sudden death was not unlike many others in my generation. Since death could come suddenly and at any moment, we lived life in the fast lane, and "lived for today." Death was car accidents, drug overdoses, war and disasters. I didn't have any experience with natural process of dying.

There was also was a phenomenon happening among older Americans that took the experience of natural death out of our family homes. Older people retired and started moving to retirement communities with warm weather, group meals, on-call doctors, and group activities. Seniors without the means to do that were also being moved out of the family home, into a new business called "nursing homes."

For many young people like myself, getting old meant getting ready to die, and assisting people at the end of their lives became a business that someday, somewhere, somehow, someone else would be paid to do. I never thought about how I would act or react as my own family and relatives approached old age and death. And I never considered that there might be a period of preparation for death, since all I ever experienced were quick, unprepared-for deaths.

Oddly enough, my first "family" death came when my husband's father died. Once again, it was sudden. He had just retired, seemed healthy and was looking forward to relaxing after a lifetime of work. But one evening he felt very dizzy, so he was put in the hospital for tests. No one realized the severity of the situation, and he died of an aneurysm in the hospital the next day. We had never been called to the hospital since doctors assured the family that he was ok, and was just being admitted for tests. So once again, someone I knew, and had grown very fond of, just suddenly was no longer there. There hadn't been any final words, no goodbyes. It was a hard time for me, but it was absolutely devastating for my husband. I felt his pain but was not equipped to help him grieve.

And so there I was, now in my late 20's and had never had the experience of being with someone as they approached a natural death. And by natural, I mean either through old age or disease. I never witnessed or shared in the phase of life where there is an understanding that life is going to come to an end soon. I certainly never considered that death could also be a time of joy or healing. And I didn't know that healing emotionally and spiritually is what's most needed at the time when physically healing is no longer a reality. I needed to learn that part of our journey is to help our loved ones prepare physically, emotionally and, what I now feel is most important, spiritually as they move towards death. I didn't understand that most deaths aren't sudden, and that most people experience a final stage of life that is their natural passage from this life to the next phase of their soul's journey.

I also didn't have much experience with elderly persons, having had only one grandparent who I didn't see very often. I realize now that since my father's parents had died when he was still a teenager, his childhood trauma kept him from talking about death.

My mother's mother also died before I was born. So I didn't have either the experiences or the lessons that grandparents bring to their families.

In his eighties, my only grandfather moved to Florida to retire so we didn't see him very often. Eventually, when he showed signs of senility and his eyesight was failing he moved back so my mother could help take care of him. He lived out his life in a nursing home. Only then, when he was in his nineties did I start to witness the slowing down, the disorientation and the separation that surrounds death. I only saw him once in awhile, and it was uncomfortable. It was uncomfortable for all of us because we hadn't learned how to be with someone whose eyes and memory were failing, who sometimes didn't recognize us, and who got depressed and slept a lot. And it was uncomfortable because we simply didn't understand the natural stages of dying that he was going through.

Often what we don't understand or are afraid of, we avoid. I'm thankful the world has changed and now there are so many informative books written by hospice nurses, geriatric professionals, people who have had near death experiences and spiritual writers. It's sad for me to realize that there was very little effort on my part to connect with my grandfather, but I didn't know how. Instead I only dutifully visited with him occasionally He went through the stages of death in the nursing home, with only my mother at his side when she could be. And finally, in his late nineties, he died in his sleep. And once again, I found out with a phone call. Just like all the other deaths before him, it felt sudden. I know now it wasn't sudden at all, and it saddens me that I didn't know at that time how to *be* with him. There was ample opportunity to connect, remember, laugh, journey, and say goodbye. But I didn't.

Even so, at that time I was given a spiritual gift. At my grandfather's burial I first got the "feeling" of him being there without his body. I "felt" him go by as we stood at the graveside in the warm summer sun. Then I "smelled" him standing near me. It was strange. It was comforting. I knew he was there, and I knew he was letting us know he was ok. It may indeed have been the beginning of my spiritual awareness. I shared the experience with my sister and she had experienced the same thing! I kept thinking about it and tried to perceive him again as days passed. But I never did. So life went on.

"Beyond the door
There's peace I'm sure
And I know there'll be no more
Tears in heaven"

Tears in Heaven, lyrics by Eric Clapton

6

My Father's Gift

It was during my birthday celebration in 1999 that the biggest change in my life began. At that time I was still working in corporate America as a photographer and audio-visual producer. Energy work and healing was not yet part of my world. I was busy juggling all the tasks of mother and stepmother, wife, daughter, and busy professional.

So it was a welcome treat to be having a special dinner in an Italian restaurant, with my husband and daughter, my sister and her family, and my mom and dad. Dad was sitting next to me. He was eighty years old, and still the funniest and sweetest man I'd ever known. He and my mom had been married for over fifty years and they now enjoyed a life filled with family, golf, travel and music.

In his seventies, dad had suffered a stroke. It was minor in severity, and his physical body recovered quickly. However, he was now slower, sometimes depressed, and often tired. He had retired from playing music professionally, except to teach trumpet lessons in the high schools. Throughout that decade, his life changed dramatically and he went from being my energetic, always busy father, to grandpa — a sweet grandfather who loved his grandchildren, but was slowing down and losing some of his zest for life. I was glad I lived close by so that we all still shared in each other's lives and spent a lot of time together. I was now learning how to witness and be supportive of the aging process.

Sometimes, dad would "nod out" for a moment or two, especially in the evening. So at first no one was alarmed when in the middle of my birthday dinner, dad's eyes closed and his head drooped down a bit. But when the momentary nod lingered and he appeared to be sleeping, I asked my mom, "does he often just fall asleep like this?"

My mom seemed a little concerned, so I shook my father's shoulder and tried to wake him. He wouldn't wake up. We panicked. The next few moments of asking the restaurant to call 911, the heart pounding fright of not knowing what to do, and the reactions of other restaurant patrons all seemed like it was happening in slow motion.

Finally, the paramedics got there. They laid him on the floor while they hooked him up to oxygen, and then put him on a stretcher to move him to the ambulance. Mom got in the ambulance, my husband took my daughter home, and I drove alone to meet the ambulance at the hospital. I don't even remember driving there. But before long, I was at the Emergency Room.

I ran into the hospital, but he hadn't arrived! How could that be? I went back out to my car and waited for the ambulance to arrive. Five minutes, ten minutes, fifteen minutes, I waited. In a panic, I finally went back inside and asked the ER people if they knew what had happened to the ambulance. They explained that the ambulance wouldn't begin the drive to the hospital until they had him stabilized. They were "working" on him. I thought that meant that something had gone wrong in the ambulance... he wasn't reviving. Why were they working on him for so long? In those fifteen or twenty minutes I suddenly realized that this might again be the way death always was for me. Sudden. No time to say goodbye.

Finally the ambulance pulled up and I ran over to it. When they opened the door, I saw dad sitting up sipping some juice, and looking quite content! Mom was sitting next to him, chatting away with the paramedics. I was livid! How could they let me sit there for so long thinking he had died! And now they were all laughing and smiling. As we moved into the hospital, one of the paramedics explained that it's not uncommon for older people to pass out. The important thing is to get them onto the floor so they can breath more easily. He also said that although it was probably "nothing serious" they would most likely keep him for tests overnight.

Something in me changed that night. Even with calming words, and dad looking better, somehow, I *knew* that he had begun his end-of-life journey. I don't know how I knew that that, but I did, and I was right. That night, I stayed up and wrote a poem to my father. I'm not a poet, and I had never written poetry before, but the language of loving memories needed to pour out of me and onto paper. The next day when he was home I shared the poem with him. I wanted him to know NOW how much I'd always loved him.

I'd always been very close with my dad. Laughter, hugs, thoughts and stories were easily shared. But the thing I loved most about my father was how we could just *be* together. No words were needed. We could communicate on a different level. But this time was different. Just *being* with him wasn't communicating what I felt. I needed him to read my words.

The next afternoon I sat with my father and asked him to read my poem. As he read my words, tears came to his eyes. I had poured my feelings onto paper through memory and prose, and that began the journey of being with my father in a new and different way than we had before. No, I did not yet know how to help him with energy work or spiritual connections. What I did know was that the most helpful thing I could now start doing for my father was to spend as much time with him as I could. So I spent the next nine months "being" with my dad during the special times, mundane times, TV times, vacation times, hospital times, and dying times. The journey had begun.

My dad started looking older more rapidly, his energy shifted into low gear, and he seemed to have lost his spark. Even though other family members and I kept looking for holistic health solutions, new hobbies, or destinations to give dad back his zest for life... somehow I knew his life on earth was coming to a close. After all, this was the man who always said, "When I can't play my music anymore, I don't want to be here." So be it.

In early spring I convinced my parents to take a vacation to Jamaica with my daughter and me. At first dad laughed at the idea and said he didn't feel up to it. But when I pointed out that he could sit around in chilly Chicago not doing much of anything except waiting for winter to be over, or he could fly with us to Jamaica, sit by the ocean drinking Blue Mountain coffee, eating fresh papaya, and watching his granddaughter play in the water... the decision was made. What the hell, he'd even treat himself to some Rum Punch or a Margarita!

We made special arrangements for wheelchairs at the airports, first floor rooms and the early seating for meals. Our days were filled with short strolls on the beach and long naps in the shade. We enjoyed tropical drinks, fresh fruits, fish, jerk chicken, lobsters and vitamin pills. He played card games with his granddaughter, and watched her swim in the ocean. We created wonderful new memories. And let's not forget those sunsets! Ya Mon!

By late spring, I had put together my first photo exhibition. I had been a photographer for more than twenty years and yet I felt this intense need to show my work in a gallery so my father could see my work while he was still alive. Awareness of his mortality awakened my own sense of time and accomplishment. As I looked over my twenty-five years of photographic work, I became aware of my own trends and patterns as a person and an artist. In some ways, as my father's artistic expression slowed down, mine blossomed. And when I finally hung the show and had my first photo opening, my mother and father were first to arrive. And despite his fatigue, Dad proudly spent the entire day with me.

I think that day was the first day that I really saw my father as an old man. Friends and family relatives that came to the gallery mentioned how frail and weakened my father looked. Photos taken that day proved it. My big, strong dad was now smaller, grayer and wrinkled. He hunched over, and spent most of the day just sitting. His energy softened, and his laughter was not quite as loud. He had become more of an observer of life than the active participant. It was interesting, and somehow sad to watch.

By early summer, I could feel his energy slipping away, so I started spending even more time with him. Sunday breakfasts. A Chicago street fair. An Indian Pow Wow. And there were more days of coming over on my days off or for dinner, to just *be* with my dad. Later in the summer we went to the Botanic Gardens. He was now so frail, that the only way he could get around was for us to push him in a wheelchair, which made him unhappy. We'd stop at the flowers and smell them together. We rested in the Japanese gardens. And I finally embraced the cycle of life… of caring for a parent, the same way he cared for me when I was a child.

By late July dad got really feeble. He would fall. Doctors had given him some medication that within days made him delusional and disoriented. They had over-medicated and mixed drugs that weren't compatible, so my family was now very unhappy with western medicine. Doctors didn't find anything particularly wrong with him other than he was getting old, but they kept putting him on medications anyway. We eventually got him off most medications, but he wasn't ever quite right after the delusional episodes, and worse, he was depressed. My mother was always very knowledgeable about vitamins, foods and natural remedies, and she continued to investigate ways to help my father. For a while dad was doing a little better with acupuncture and Chinese herbs. But eventually he had another episode so we went to the hospital for more tests, and he remained there for several weeks.

He was now in a hospital that had an older clientele, and the service and kindness was much better. There was more understanding of the health stages that elderly people go through, instead of the frenzy of doctors trying to fix everything at all cost. I would come by after work and *be* with him as much as I could. But it started to change. He didn't like me touching his hands, or worse, climbing in the bed next to him to snuggle. He was agitated and hurting… all perfectly normal stages, I now know. But at the time, I couldn't understand why human closeness was not helping or comforting him.

Additionally, there were times when he needed help with bodily functions, or he couldn't communicate his needs. We both found this frustrating and embarrassing. As the days went on, I realized I could be there physically, but I didn't know how to be with my father spiritually. I was losing my connection to my dad, (or so I thought) and that was the most painful part for me.

Finally, the hospital said they couldn't continue to keep him there unless he actively participated in therapy. But dad wasn't participating. He wanted to rest, not exercise. And the hospital also couldn't keep him there unless they were administering some sort of medical treatment. Since he had little appetite, the only thing they *could* do was give him a feeding tube. If he didn't want a feeding tube, there was no reason for him to be there.

I remember sitting in the hallway with my father, holding his hand and explaining to him that they wanted to insert a feeding tube and he'd have to stay "hooked up" to some machines. I asked him if he wanted to do that, or would he rather we bring him home. *Home.* Home to his wife. Home where he could hold the dog on his lap. Home to his own family room with the TV, and the baseball games, and the warm August breezes blowing through the windows. Home where friends and family could visit, say goodbye, laugh, play music, and all *be* together. And what was still unsaid, but understood by both of us, come home to die. He cried a little at the decision. But he nodded and said he wanted to go home. And so we brought him home.

I am grateful that my family didn't start searching through all sorts of medical answers to try *anything and everything* to prolong his life. Even though I think my mother thought that once he was back home and out of the hospital he'd get new strength and rebound... I understood that he was ready. And this is a big part of the lesson... accepting and knowing when someone is ready to die. Dad was only eighty-one, which, in today's world didn't seem very old.

I had no idea how long the process might be, but I was pretty sure it wouldn't be long. So over the next few days, we welcomed in some of his best friends, relatives, and his beloved trumpet students who played music for him. Nighttime nurses came to keep him comfortable. And we sat with him round the clock.

Just like a pregnancy, we had spent nine months preparing to birth my father back to spirit. Nine months of getting him prepared to let go of this world and fall into the peaceful and loving heart of the spirit world... back into the arms of his mother and father who he'd been without since he was a teenager and all the others who patiently awaited his return to the other side. And almost nine months to the day, when he was ready, he did just that.

Five days after bringing him home, after a day of sitting with Dad watching him go in and out of consciousness, I left for a dinner break and Mom went up for a short nap. A nurse sat quietly in another room. And at some miraculous, quiet moment, my father decided to let go, release his spirit and die peacefully... by himself.

"Softly,
I will leave you softly
For my heart would break,
if you should wake and see me go"

Softly as I Leave You, lyrics by
Giorgio Calabrese, Antonio DeVita, Hal Shaper

This is the poem I wrote for my father. I share this although I am fully aware that I am not a poet, and this may break every rule of prose/poetry writing. It doesn't matter. I wrote from my heart and I encourage you write or speak from your hearts, too. That IS all that matters.

"My Little Daddy"

I used to call you "My Little Daddy."
    We thought it was funny
    and weren't sure why.

Maybe it was left-over memory of once-upon-a-time, when
    as one part of the cycle, I was the older.
    Today, like then, I sometimes want to hold your face
    and say,
    "I'm so proud of you"
    with the feeling of both parent and child.

Maybe you were my "Little Daddy" because even all dressed up
    in your tuxedo, tall and handsome, off to the adult world of work
    you always stopped long enough to snuggle
    and hold me and say
    "I love you."

You let it be safe, and warm and fun for me
    to be your little girl.

I don't think it was foreshadowing of now,
    when 80-odd years have caused you to physically
    grow so small.
    Because in my mind and heart,
    You are the tallest of men.

You aren't just the big, strong head of the family,
  the Dad.
  You are so Cool!

Last night I sat and looked and listened to the 3 trumpeters playing
  Tribute to Sinatra and the Big Band Sound,
  while being reminded of the world You lived and worked in.
  Those trumpeters were being YOU....
  You were the big band...
  you did play Sinatra and Sammy and...

And when your evening was done,
  after you made all the people dance,
  and smile,
  You would come home to us.

When I was small I remember you carrying me from your Big bed
  into my small bed.
  I'd hug you and smell the party left on your clothes...
  the aftershave, smoke, sweat...
  licorice mints from Mangam's Chateau.
  I'd fall back to sleep, secure.

And when I was older, you'd come in, kiss the dog,
  bring in the hot bagels,
  and we'd sit and eat and you'd listen
  to reports of my dates.
  Then we'd watch the end of a movie 'til 2am.

I've always liked just sitting with you.
  Whether watching TV,
  listening to you tell stories at family gatherings, or you
  snoozing in your chair while I snoozed on the couch.

I've always loved to just Be with you.
    We don't even have to say anything.
    We just Be.

Maybe that's why I used to call you my "Little Daddy" –
    because somehow, from the time I was small, I could feel the
    quiet
    peaceful
    love you had for me.

It's always been that little piece of you,
    your sometimes overwhelming love, so huge
    yet small enough to live inside my heart…
    the little piece of you that will always be inside of me
    forever and ever.

Maybe as a child, my calling you my "Little Daddy" was my
    way of saying "I Love You" before I even realized
    what that meant.

I love you Daddy.

7

A Change of Spiritual Perception

I remember getting the call that my dad had passed. Even with all the preparation and knowing his time was getting close, I never thought he'd leave when we weren't sitting there holding his hands. I'd only left for an hour to go home for dinner. I couldn't believe I didn't get to spend his last moments with him. It was not how I had imagined.

I barely remember driving back to my mother's house, but when I walked in the most fascinating thing happened. I could *feel* my dad there. I guess I could feel his energy. It wasn't that small, feeble, weak, sickly feeling that had surrounded him for weeks. It was big. It was the wonderful strong, youthful, Father energy that I remembered from when I was a kid coming home from school and even without seeing him, I knew he was there. It was a magical feeling that he was free of his body, and his spirit was soaring. It was beautiful.

Then things got confusing. My mother was grief stricken. The nurse was trying to calm her. After all this "preparation" the moment had arrived… was I really prepared? A hospice volunteer showed up just a few minutes later. She hadn't been there to help us with the death, but she was a godsend to help my mom begin to understand the process of what to do next.

I walked into the family room where my father lay in the bed. His face finally looked relaxed and peaceful, but Dad didn't seem to be in there. It was so strange to see him lifeless, yet somehow sweet to see the calmness. All the tension had left his face. I touched his physical body knowing it would be for the last time. And I was fully aware that I had just entered into a realm of the unknown that was at the same time natural and scary. The moment of losing my parent, friend and creator of my life and heart had arrived. I was aware that I was putting up an emotional wall, my way of "keeping it together." I needed to breathe, so I went out to the backyard. When my sister arrived, she came into the yard and confirmed what I had been feeling. Dad's spirit was there. He was out there with his girls... we could feel him... we knew.

I remembered from years ago, standing at my grandfather's graveside, slightly and momentarily aware of a presence or a smell. Now I really understood and savored this special moment of awareness that broke through the veil of our physical reality and the spiritual world. I didn't try to understand, I just embraced and enjoyed the moment. My dad *WAS* there with us... I could feel him.

Throughout the next few months I realized that one of the ways I perceive spirit is through smell. Just as I *smelled* my grandfather at his funeral, I would now smell trumpet oil! As a child, I used to love to watch the intricate process of taking the trumpet apart and oiling the valves. It fascinated me. For months after my father died, I would suddenly and surprisingly smell trumpet oil. Nothing else smells just like that. Then one day I was looking at a pair of sunglasses that my dad had bought when we were together at a street fair. As I opened the case, I could smell his aftershave. It was so comforting and I knew my mother would love to share that with me. But when she opened the case, she couldn't smell a thing! Neither could my sister. Was I more sensitive, or was Dad using smell to communicate with me alone? All I know is that these smells didn't come when I was thinking about my father. Instead they would just happen out of the blue, or perhaps when it was his intent to connect with me. I found that comforting.

The first few months after his death, I was pretty comfortable with what had been my role at the end of my father's life. I knew I had done my best to be with and comfort my dad for the last nine months. I felt grateful that we brought him home to die surrounded by family and friends. I was accepting that he had lived a wonderful life and left without a great deal of illness or pain. And although I felt blessed with moments when I felt like he was somehow "here," I had a hard time accepting that the loss of spiritual connection was a normal part of death. I tried to convince myself that "that's just how it is... that is death."

After six months of grieving and getting our lives back to normal, instead of feeling better I still had a gnawing frustration that the ability to connect with my dad had diminished during his last few months of life, and now it was completely gone. Eventually I also lost the ability to feel him around me. There were no more whiffs of trumpet oil or aftershave... it was all just memory, and I knew a piece that should have been nurtured while he was still alive, was missing.

Why does that happen? Why doesn't anyone teach us how to stay spiritually connected to someone even as they lay dying? I became depressed. I felt unfulfilled at work. I kept feeling pushed to understand more about this transition time. Then, one afternoon, while sitting in my chiropractors office, I saw a sign for Reiki class. I'd never heard of Reiki energy healing. "What's Reiki?" I asked.

"Oh, you'll love it" the receptionist answered. She also happened to be a Reiki Master and would be co-teaching the Reiki class on the weekend. "We still have room for one more, come join us."

I guess that's all I needed to hear. It would be a weekend of training for the first level of Japanese hands-on energy healing. So without really knowing what it was, without checking my schedule, or checking with my family or checking what it would cost, I heard myself say, "OK, I'll be there what time does it start?"

Another life journey had begun for me.

"Peace, sweet peace will come, I know
...the passion is understanding,
kindness is the key."

Peace Will Come, lyrics by Terry Diers

8

My Reiki Journey Begins

I found learning about and experiencing energy work fascinating. I also was not very good at it... at first. I had been so visually focused my whole life that learning to *feel* instead of to *see*, just wasn't happening. And yet, I kept working at it because the world of the unseen just might hold the key to understanding how to be connected to others and, more importantly, connected to God, Spirit, our Higher Self. The name didn't matter.

In Reiki I learned new techniques to quiet my mind and exercises to feel the subtleties of the human energy field. We received "attunements" which is a process of opening up the energy centers at the crown of the head, the heart, and the palms of the hands. This system, unique to Reiki, is how the healing energy is channeled through the body of the healer, out through the hands and into the body or energy field of the person in need of healing. I learned the techniques of hand placements for treating specific organs and conditions of the body, and how to move stuck or negative energies away from the body.

As I practiced I began to "feel" the warm, relaxing flow of the energy move through my body and out through my hands. I did Reiki on myself and could relieve headaches or I'd feel the warmth soothe sore and achy muscles in my own body. And I was thrilled when the people I was working on began to give me feedback. Some people could feel the energy move through their bodies. Pains went away. They slept better. Others got so relaxed during treatments that they could "hear" the answers to the issues they were working on and became aware of their own guidance. Eventually, with more practice, I began to perceive both the energy movement and the reactions it was creating. I was "opening up" as they say… using senses and perceptions that were always there, but never used. And oh, how I wished I had known how to do these techniques during the time my father was dying. It was fascinating on so many levels that I decided to take the next level of training to learn about emotional healing and use the "symbols" of Reiki that make the healing more powerful. The physical, mental and spiritual aspects of healing work all came together.

I was also realizing that what is taught in Reiki is really just the techniques to allow people to do their own healing… that energy workers are only the channel. We don't do the healing. What we call the universal life force energy, also referred to as spiritual energy, works with the person and their higher selves. We just help the process… we are the connector cables, the on switch and quality control to be sure that people are in a safe, nurturing energy that allows them to do their physical, emotional and spiritual work. We call this holding space, and I believe it is the most important thing we do.

I also had to wrap my head around the idea that energy healing can go beyond the limits of time and space. We could heal the traumas of past events, and also send healing energy to future events. But more importantly, we could send healing to others that aren't physically present with us. This was quite a new concept for me. Perhaps this was another way to stay connected to our loved ones as they approach their deaths. We could both send healing energy and feel a person's energy without being physically with them. I had finally discovered a way to stay spiritually and physically connected to someone and I wondered how that would have changed the experience with my father.

The unseen world of energy was magical to me. It opened me up to new considerations about how our thoughts and intentions create the world around us. And it showed me that the unseen can be felt and perceived in ways I had never considered. I knew I wanted to take the Reiki Master classes, but my teacher wanted me to wait almost a year, to keep practicing and developing both my awareness and my technique. Finally, almost two years after my father's death, and a week after our country had just gone through the trauma of 9/11, I began my Master Class.

That class was an insightful, healing and spiritual journey that took over a year to complete. Besides learning the higher levels of Reiki, we got lessons about creating a place to journey within our own heart centers, techniques for creating a sacred visualization to connect with our own guides and angels and were introduced to other modalities like quantum touch, moxa bustion, past-life regression, aromatherapy, nutrition and much more. In being introduced to so many other modalities and techniques, it began to open up the world of healing to see how it's all connected. Not all Reiki classes are taught that way, so I felt very lucky to have this very broad education in the healing arts.

I continued to practice Reiki on friends and family, and started seeing some clients. I found that I liked to take them through short meditations or journeys as we started their treatments. At first I would focus mostly on physical healing. I would have people visualize a healing light and have them breathe it down through every part of their body. I also began to use some other guided meditation techniques I had learned at a Cancer Wellness Center and realized how much more powerful they became during a Reiki session. And I was learning to listen to my own guidance, directing me to say new and different things to help people meditate or journey into their own healing experiences. I also read many books about souls, spirituality and reincarnation... anything that might give me more insight beyond my own limited views. I believe this was laying the foundation for work that was to come later when I started doing hospice.

One day during one of my Reiki classes, my teacher told me to send Reiki to my father. My father? How silly was that! He was already dead... he didn't need healing. He was with Spirit, God, his relatives, the Angels. Why would he need MY healing sent to him?

"Because all beings, no matter where they are on their journey, in a physical body or in spirit, always love and appreciate healing energy being sent to them," my teacher said, "and it will help you connect with your father."

Wow. Finally. Connect. It was more than two years since his death, and now there was something I could actually do to connect with my father. Send him healing. What a beautiful idea. And even though years had passed, I knew that when it came to sending healing energy, time and space meant nothing. It was now, in this moment that I could do something to connect to my dad. I had experienced enough Reiki to know that even if *I* didn't feel anything, the white light, love and healing that I was sending would be received by my father.

So by sending healing energy, I would be connecting. And by connecting, I would be healing myself.

"Now you know why you took this class," my teacher said. "Send love to your father." And so I did.

> *"I am that warm voice in the cold wind that whispers*
> *And if you listen you'll hear me call across the sky*
> *As long as I still can reach out and touch you*
> *Then I will never die"*

> **Remember Me** lyrics by
> James Horner and Cynthia Weil

9

My First Hospice Patient

I began taking time to send healing to my father. I felt so good sending him energy. It felt like a prayer with more action. We all pray for, or talk to our loved ones who are no longer with us. And yet this was different, I was giving back to the man who had given me so much. I was still showing him my love in a way that I knew he was receiving.

And yet, I still wanted to learn more about staying connected during the actual time of death. I wanted to see if doing Reiki on someone would make the dying experience more meaningful, more participatory, more comforting. I volunteered to do hospice work. And that's how I met Charlie. Charlie was my first hospice patient.

I will never forget him. He knew nothing about Reiki and I knew little about walking into the room of a complete stranger to give physical and spiritual comfort. Besides not knowing what his physical condition would be, I wondered what it would be like to spend an hour with a man who already knew and accepted that he was nearing his final days on earth.

Charlie was in a nursing home. Since he was not in his own home, I was expecting that he would be quite ill, bedridden perhaps. I was surprised when I saw a man, only in his late sixties that, except for wearing an oxygen mask, looked pretty healthy, could get out of the bed and walk around. He was very alert and conversational. He was lying in bed next to a window that overlooked a parking lot. There was a picture of Jesus hanging over his head, and a corkboard with pictures of a few children and grandchildren tacked to it.

His brother was also in the room, sitting near his feet. I introduced myself and set about my routine of plugging in a CD player and laying a few crystals near a candle. I knew I could not light the candle with oxygen in the room, but for the moment, the routine gave me comfort and some time to get over my nerves. His brother chose to leave, although I told him he was welcome to stay. In retrospect, I'm glad Charlie and I began our journey alone.

I remember our first conversation. Charlie told me he hadn't a clue what Reiki was, but that through hospice he could sign up for several different healing modalities. Since he didn't have a lot of visitors, he signed up to receive as many hospice services as they would allow! I laughed, pulled up a chair next to him and gave him a basic explanation of what Reiki is all about. He thought for a few moments, and then quietly spoke. He said that he was a Catholic and had never heard of healing energy in the context of the Universal Life Force Energy. Then he pointed above his head to the picture of Jesus and said, "I hope he doesn't mind."

I smiled, took his hand and said, "Well, I'm not a Catholic, but knowing how Jesus dedicated his life to spreading the healing light, I'm pretty sure he'd approve."

Charlie laughed. I then added, "and if lightning suddenly strikes, I promise I'll stop!"

Then we talked a little more about Reiki being a method of healing that would help him to relax and help relieve any pain he might be in. Although I tried to keep it light, I realized immediately that my conversation carried a lot of responsibility: to the Reiki community, to the hospice that included energy workers as part of their offering, and especially to the patients who came from all different religious backgrounds. It was my first lesson in learning to allow Reiki to not only flow through my hands, but to tap into my heart energy for answers. I learned not to speak until I felt that I was speaking from my heart or being guided by a higher source.

Charlie had pulmonary fibrosis. He wasn't in pain, but his breathing was difficult and I could hear his breath gurgle deep in his chest. I began by placing my hands directly on his chest. He liked the warm feeling and within about five minutes, the noise of his breathing quieted down. I was rather surprised myself, having never worked on this type of physical ailment. Inside I was so excited, I was really seeing Reiki "work." I was hoping the Reiki would be of some comfort, and indeed it was.

Next I set about doing a full body treatment as best I could with his hospital bed up against the wall. This was my first lesson into "uncomfortable" Reiki, finding it hard to get into the proper positions. Although I knew I could just sit and hold his hand, or beam the energy at him, I really wanted him to feel the comforting warmth of my hands over his entire body, so I leaned over the bed as long as I could, holding each Reiki position.

During this time I began to learn a lot about Charlie – his life, his work, his wife and his children. But the most surprising thing to me was that although his lungs were showing the effect of his disease, he still had at least six months to live, maybe more. At that time, I was pretty naïve and thought hospice was for patients in the last few days or weeks of their life. In training we learned that people begin hospice at all different stages of illness. So Charlie, knowing he was terminal and wouldn't live more than six to nine months, had decided to bring in the comfort of hospice workers as soon as possible. So the journey with my first hospice patient had begun.

We did indeed have six months together. I would be going through all the stages with this man and his family — putting to use the lessons and gifts that Reiki had taught me. In one hour, once-a-week visits, all those moments of frustration and feeling helpless at my father's side, were now returning as lessons. I was to learn to handle those situations in new ways. The lessons of acting from love, not fear, were now to be learned with a family I had never known before. The lessons of compassion, patience, responsibility, and acceptance were at hand. I was expecting to practice only the physical application of Reiki. Spirit had other plans for me.

The lessons kept coming. Kindness. Listening. Choosing music. Knowing when to joke. Knowing when a guided meditation would "feel" better than hands-on Reiki. Knowing when to be quiet. And knowing when to just *be* with someone. It's really an honor to be sitting at the bedside of someone during their final journey in life. Being included in that special time, whether or not we know the person intimately is a very sacred act. And I embraced every visit.

There were several things that really stood out in my memory. The first was that Charlie was able to spend less time on his oxygen after the first couple of Reiki treatments. His morphine dose was also lessened because he was feeling more comfortable for longer periods of time. And even in later stages when his oxygen was kept flowing all the time, we could unhook it during the Reiki, and for those wonderful hours, he breathed easily. I kept wishing that one of his family members would learn to do energy work so that Charlie could get daily Reiki, not just weekly.

Another time my back was really bothering me when I tried to lean over the bed. I would usually spend most of my time at his chest and lungs, but this time I spent more time on his legs and feet so that I could sit. My hands were surrounding his calves when he commented, "How did you know that would feel so good right there?"

I was actually a little surprised at how well he responded to the energy work on his legs. It was a reminder to focus energy to all parts of the body. He wondered how I always knew *exactly* where he was feeling discomfort. I believe the truth was simply that the warmth of Reiki hands felt good *everywhere*. He hardly walked or moved around much anymore and all his muscles were in need of stimulation.

As weeks passed there were times when I came to Charlie's room and he needed to be cleaned up physically or needed to relieve himself. Staff was short, and Charlie was uncomfortable, so I learned to take care of him. Situations that both my father and I had found embarrassing, took on a different perspective. I found the rewards of helping outweighed the uneasiness of being with someone as their independence was lessened daily. I was beginning to act from my heart and my spirit in ways that, although I loved him dearly, I couldn't do for my father.

My last visit with Charlie was very special, although I didn't realize at the time that it would be the last. I had tried to cancel my visit because I was going to be leaving town the next day to spend the Christmas holidays in New Mexico. My husband and I were taking a driving trip with three of our kids, and I needed the time to pack and organize. I requested a replacement from the hospice, but they couldn't find one. The next day, the hospice called to tell me that Charlie was very disappointed that I was cancelling, and he had asked if he could see me once more before the Christmas holidays. I couldn't refuse.

By then Charlie had been moved into a private room. He didn't get out of bed anymore, and was moving in and out of consciousness. As I approached the room I could hear his wife talking loudly on her cell phone relaying a blow-by-blow accounting of his condition to whoever was on the other end of the line. It was loud, disturbing and I could just feel how disconnected she was from her husband at this point. His brother was also in the room and his anxiety was overwhelming. I took a deep breath as I entered. My intention was to bring some calm into the room. As I approached Charlie's bed I could see that he was either unconscious or sleeping deeply, but once he sensed me there, he extended his hand to me. His eyes remained closed, but I could see a faint smile.

His wife became excited that he was moving, and chattered even louder on the phone. "Oh look, he's reaching his hand out!" she said loudly. "It's a miracle! He's waking up!" On and on she loudly spoke into the phone.

This was one of those times when I knew that Spirit was putting words in my mouth. I heard myself explain in a very calm voice that even though Charlie was unconscious or asleep a lot of the time, he was still quite aware of everyone in the room. It was time that they could be sharing together even though he wasn't always responding with words. I almost couldn't believe it was *me* telling the wife to get off the phone and *be* with her husband.

But more importantly, it was a new lesson for me. There was a lot of noise in the room, and it seemed that Charlie was asleep or unconscious. How did he know I was there? That's when I realized how aware Charlie was... that closed eyes don't necessarily mean a person is unaware of their surroundings. As Charlie reached for my hand, I knew that he was totally with us, even though his eyes remained closed. He just wanted to connect. He knew that by holding my hand he'd feel the familiar energy, the comforting touch that we had been sharing for months. He didn't need any words, he just wanted to connect with me.

His wife put down the phone and I suggested she hold his other hand. His brother, with tears in his eyes, happy that his brother was aware and moving after having been still all day, then looked at me and asked, "can you perform a miracle... can you do *something now* to make him well?"

I paused to again allow Spirit to bring the right words to my voice. I felt that longing that every energy worker feels... that moment when we wish that this would be the time that God performs a miracle through us. If only. But as quickly as that wishful feeling appeared, it vanished and other words flowed from my mouth. I found myself explaining that there was indeed a miracle happening, the miracle of being together for comfort and spiritual healing to take place. Being "healed" for Charlie, at this point, was having his brother and his wife sitting at his bedside holding his hands, free to express anything they needed or wanted to say, and just feeling the love. The healing would be in trusting the process and being able to let go.

I told them that I don't do miracles, that comes from a different realm altogether. I said it was more important that they all felt peaceful enough together to let Charlie release from this body and let his spirit be free. I wanted them to truly be present in the moment so they could hold these last days of togetherness in their hearts forever. I did Reiki at Charlie's head while his family held his hands. I told him how wonderful it was to know him, and that I would be thinking of him while I was away for a few weeks. I promised I'd see him as soon as I came back in town.

A week later I was with my family, climbing the mesa at Ojo Caliente in New Mexico. For me, Ojo Caliente is a very ancient and peaceful place. When I'm there, I feel that wisdom can be tapped into, answers come more easily and it's easy to feel my spiritual connection. I was sitting quietly on a rock, when suddenly a strange feeling came over me. Somehow I knew Charlie was there with me. And he thanked me. I can't even explain how I knew... I didn't hear it, I didn't see him, but I *knew*. I just suddenly, in my heart and in my head, knew I was being thanked. It was a profoundly beautiful feeling that I shall never forget.

When I got down from the mesa I found a place where my cell phone worked and there was a call from hospice on my phone. The message was simple. Charlie had died.

My first experience in hospice had been a beautiful experience of learning and sharing. I did not yet know how to lead people through journeys, or do soul connections, but I had helped them to all BE together... to be more aware and embrace the moments quietly and peacefully. And it was rather sweet that I had learned to enjoy spending time with someone who had been a complete stranger to me – helping him embrace his final journey.

Charlie visited me from time to time. Again, I don't know exactly how to put into words how I knew when he was there, but I knew. He became one of my teachers to whom I am grateful. And once when I "felt" Charlie around, he sent me the most wonderful message I ever received. He communicated with me in such a clear way that I know he said, "Your father would be very proud of you."

I knew then that my time with Charlie was both a beautiful gift and a healing.

"As strong as you were, tender you go.
I'm watching you breathing for the last time.
A song for your heart, but when it is quiet,
I know what it means and I'll carry you home."

Carry You Home lyrics by
James Blount, Max Martin

10

Silent Lessons

My next Hospice experience was quite different. I was sent to the private home of Mrs. Adams. Her daughter, Betty, a woman about my age had been caring for Mrs. Adams for more than two years. Now, I was told, she was very near death. Betty had requested someone to do Reiki, in addition to her hospice care.

For me, it was the first time I would go into a family home for a hospice visit. It was a lovely old home in a beautiful tree-lined neighborhood. After six months of going to a nursing home this was a welcomed change. As we did for my father, a bed had been set up in Mrs. Adam's living room so her daughter could spend time with her without being confined to a small bedroom. The room was filled with beautiful art, framed pictures of loved ones and antiques all around.

Betty was quiet and reserved. There was a peaceful acceptance about her. She had made the decision to quit her job and live in her mother's house acting as her caregiver for the rest of her mother's life. I found this dedication to her mother's care to be a beautiful final gift to her mother.

Betty brought me to her mother's bedside. She was unconscious, totally motionless, pale and thin, with very shallow breathing. She was in no pain, and looked peaceful so I knew the treatment would be more about comfort and spiritual connection. She hadn't eaten any solid food in more than a week and was only taking small amounts of water.

I decided to scan her body before I started. Scanning is a process we do in Reiki to feel for heat, tingling or other disturbances in the energy that surrounds the physical body. They can be areas of injury, organs that aren't functioning properly, or areas of inflammation and pain. The way the energy around the body feels gives energy workers information as to what areas are in need of healing and balancing.

I also feel the energy centers of the body. These energy centers run from the top of the head to the base of the spine, each one relating to a different set of emotional and spiritual issues. For example, when someone is dealing with issues of love or lack of it, it is the heart center located in the chest that may go out of balance. Or if someone loses their job and they are worried about survival issues, the energy center at the base of the spine may be affected. Questions about life purpose, God, or higher-self affect the energy center at the crown of the head. These emotional issues start in the energy centers, but can eventually cause physical disturbances in the body. In eastern studies these energy centers are called chakras, defined as wheels of spinning energy, and there are many modalities that revolve around balancing the chakra system, opening shut down areas, and aligning the chakras. In a healthy person the goal is to have all these energy centers open and balanced.

In the case of someone who is very close to death, the lower energy centers which have to do with issues of security, survival, family and belonging are usually in the process of shutting down and the upper energy centers which are the spiritual and psychic centers of the body open up to connect with and embrace spiritual messages. Simply stated we begin to let go of our connection to the earth and embrace the non-physical world of spirit. Since Mrs. Adams spent most of her time unconscious, which I interpreted as spending time in the spiritual realm, I expected that when I scanned her spiritual and intuitive energy centers, they would be very open and active. But they were not. I was quite surprised when I could feel very little energy there, and instead her lower energy centers, the ones having to do with day to day issues, personal power, creativity, and desires of the inner child, were still very open and active. It didn't make sense to me. Mrs. Adams was still very grounded... I wondered why.

I took my place at her head and began sending energy into her third eye. Betty sat with us, holding her mother's hand. As I let the Reiki flow, Betty began speaking with me. She said she and her mother were very close. Mrs. Adams was an artist and spent her life creating beautiful things. Until recently, they had been able to communicate easily, and but now she was sad that her mother no longer spoke. I understood how she felt. Without adding any suggestions, I just continued to do the Reiki and with no words from me. Eventually Betty began to understand her mother's communication.

I found it fascinating. I watched and listened as the two women communicated without any words. In the relaxing calm of the flow of energy, I was witnessing a connection I had never experienced before... the connection I would eventually learn to facilitate. I could feel it in my heart and sense it in my crown. Although I felt that my first hospice patient, Charlie, had sent me some communication, I never was aware of a connection between him and his family. This was different. In the calm and peaceful energy of acceptance, Betty and Mrs. Adams were connecting.

My impression was that as Mrs. Adam's time of death drew closer, Betty continued to stay close and stay connected, not wanting her mother to leave. This was literally keeping her mother alive. She had never given her mother permission to leave or reassured her mother that she would be fine without her. Betty wasn't ready to let her go and so Mrs. Adams was staying alive as long as she possibly could. Now it made perfect sense why her lower energy centers were keeping her grounded and she was staying closed off to spirit. Mrs. Adams was fighting to stay earthbound, she spiritually wasn't ready to die.

I did some work to connect her heart and her crown to spirit, but made no verbal suggestions to either Mrs. Adams or Betty. And I also put out the intention that Betty would get enough peace and strength to finally let her mother know it was ok to go.

Whatever comfort they were getting from the Reiki, they both seemed more relaxed. So I simply helped them to create an opening for more spiritual awareness for both of them. When I left, we didn't set up another appointment, as I believed Mrs. Adams would die within the next few days. I wished them well, and set off.

I was very surprised when hospice called a week later and told me that Betty wanted me to come back! Mrs. Adams had held on another week without food, medication and very little water.

This time when I approached the bed, there was a smell of death, something I hadn't experienced before. Mrs. Adams was in the fetal position, and Betty sat at her side as if she was sitting with a baby. It was beautiful. Betty told me that that within a few days of my being there, she had finally been able to tell her mother it was ok to leave. It was time. Betty was now ready.

I again scanned her energy centers, and, not surprisingly, everything had shifted. There was very little energy in her lower energy centers, and the third eye and her crown were wide open. Her heart was open, but not totally, and I believe this was because there was still some sadness around leaving. So I worked on her heart, and did a general treatment of comfort and connecting.

Once again, Betty felt a non-verbal message from her mother that gave her much comfort. There was a wonderful serenity about that final treatment. Now, I believed, they were both ready. This time when I said goodbye, I knew I wouldn't be back and I was right. Mrs. Adams died a few days later.

I had learned another precious lesson from Mrs. Adams... and yet she had never uttered a word to me. Betty and her mother had spent a beautiful time together birthing her mother back to spirit, and now they were both setting out on their own new journeys.

I now had two very different experiences with hospice. One was long-term and one very short. One included lots of talking and physical involvement, the other was silent. I was eager to learn more. That's when the hospital that I was volunteering for decided to close their hospice doors permanently.

"Hello silence my old friend,
You've come to talk with me again"
...and whisper the sounds of silence."

Sounds of Silence, *lyrics by* Paul
Simon & Art Garfunkle

11

What Next?

It seemed another transition time in my life approached. I believe that when things end or change abruptly, it's best to take some time to analyze what's been happening and also trust that divine guidance is at work. Certainly I could have contacted another hospice and joined as a volunteer, but it seemed that there was something different that needed to happen.

My life had changed dramatically from the time of my father's death. I was still doing photography and audio-visual production work to make a living, but also knew I wanted to do more with energy work. Maybe it was time to start seeing my own clients. I set up a Reiki table in my second bedroom, and began lecturing at local libraries about the healing effects of Reiki to attract clients. I would lead groups in meditations, do Reiki demonstrations and offered energy balancing at local events. I also began writing articles about Reiki for a woman's paper in the Chicago area. Eventually I also rented space in a yoga studio. New lessons came with each new client and I loved what I was learning. I began teaching Reiki classes and my life moved to a completely new realm.

The interesting thing about energy work is that there are so many different people offering so many different techniques and methods. So I continued to go to healing meditations and signed up for more and more seminars and classes. I realized that all of them offered something unique, inspiring and valid. I spent more time learning from nature and tapping into my own inner wisdom. My life as a holistic healer, energy worker and spiritual teacher was well underway.

Instead of going back as a volunteer for hospice, I decided to start a healing circle at a hospice facility. Reiki and other energy healers gathered to give volunteer healing sessions for hospice workers, not hospice patients. I realized how emotionally stressful and energetically draining hospice work could be, so I and many of my students and Reiki friends would gather to do healing treatments for hospice volunteers and staff, and I was thrilled at how many realized the benefits of Reiki and chose to take class, as well.

When summer came, our numbers doing the Healing Circle at the hospice increased. Although our circle lasted from seven to nine p.m., on many warm summer nights you'd find groups of us still lingering in the parking lot until ten or eleven o'clock, or heading to the ice cream parlor to continue the sharing, the stories, the support and the fun.

It was that same summer, when I got the call from one of the chiropractors that I had been working for, that he had a client whose mother was dying. She had her round-the-clock nurses, and some hospice visits, but now the family was looking for a "spiritual healing session." He asked if I was interested.

I had only had two "real" hospice assignments up until then, Charlie and Mrs. Adams. But the family was asking for something different. They hadn't asked for either a Reiki treatment OR a hospice visit. What would I do? I felt myself go quiet... I was thinking. I was waiting for my answer to come. And ultimately I heard myself say, "Yes, I'll do it."

That was the warm summer day I went to visit Mrs. O'Reilly, and this new journey of doing Reiki and spiritual connections at the time of death began for me. And over the years there have been more and more beautiful moments and stories to share. Angela. Mr. Cavelli. A woman my own age who never came out of a coma after a stroke. A best friend's uncle. More family friends, and more complete strangers. And each had a beautiful individual story. I gained my confidence in sitting and journeying with people at their time of death. It was now time to learn some other important lessons.

> *"Even if your hands are shaking*
> *And your faith is broken*
> *Even as the eyes are closing*
> *Do it with a heart wide open"*

Say What You Need to Say,
lyrics by John Mayer

12

"I Want to Go Home!"

Only once have I had someone get upset in the midst of their Reiki journey. That was Darlene. A tough woman with a deep voice and sharp sense of humor, Darlene was in the final stages of lung cancer. She had had several surgeries and, since she lived alone, her family decided that after her last surgery, she was to be moved to an assisted living center. Her son and daughter-in-law were daily visitors.

Her daughter-in-law, Ann, was a friend of mine. Ann had received Reiki from me on previous occasions, and always enjoyed her treatments. Since she was spending so much time at Darlene's bedside, she thought Reiki would be a great way to get her to relax and relieve some of her pain. We were both hopeful that once she experienced the calming effects of a treatment, I could visit her several times a week.

When I arrived at the retirement home I was amazed at how lovely it was. Beautiful decorations and furniture, pretty views and a nice, upbeat feeling to it. Darlene was sitting in a chair when I arrived. She was still moving around on her own pretty well, awake much of the day, but on morphine for her pain. Although I had met her before, her greeting was rather abrupt and I knew immediately that she wasn't terribly open to the Reiki treatment.

Ann had invited me there and tried to explain to Darlene that this would be a nice, relaxing treatment for her. Some small talk and explanations of what I was going to do as I set up the CD player and arranged my oils, didn't pique much interest. She was, understandably, more interested in making sure that her morphine injection would be on time. I explained that Reiki might alleviate some of the pain, and we should just go ahead and start... but she insisted we wait for the shot. I noticed the tension in the room — especially in my friend who really wanted this to be a nice treat for her mother-in-law. Once Darlene had been given her morphine and was comfortable in her chair, I started the music and put some essential oils in my hand. I picked an oil with a mixture of essences including rose oil, geranium, bergamot and lemon... one that most people love! It's a very high vibration, soothing and uplifting.

She hated it! What a great lesson for me not to make any assumptions regarding music, lighting, conversation, candles or aromatherapy. Since I can't know what the experience is like for someone in days so close to their death, and everyone is so different, I eventually learned to ask first, to be very careful in my suggestions and to honor whatever mood the person might be in at the moment.

Since some of the oil was now on my hands... I had to be careful not to get too close to her face. I tried to stay positive and move her focus from the smell to the warmth of my hands on her shoulders as I stood behind her. I explained what she might feel, and asked her to breathe deeply and close her eyes.

About this time, I noticed my friend, in a more nervous state than I've ever seen her! She was sitting in a chair off to the side and her leg was in a non-stop frenzy of bouncing. I imagined the Reiki beaming out to envelop her in some healing light... and asked that the universal life force energy fill the entire room. I felt a shift in Darlene, and she began to relax. I also could feel my friend begin to relax. Her breathing slowed and her leg stopped bouncing. I began to move around a bit, putting energy and the Reiki love symbol into her energy field. I also used the emotional healing symbol. Finally... things were settling down and I felt the anxiety begin to melt away as the energy provided a warm, relaxing flow.

As I continued to do my treatment on the physical body, Spirit began to whisper in my ear that Darlene would now want to do some meditation and journeying. First, I wanted to get her used to following my voice and using her imagination. I had my friend sit closer to the bedside, and hold hands with Darlene. Together, we imagined the white light beaming down on their heads, providing a soothing and relaxing warmth that spread out over their entire bodies. Then I had them breathe in the healing, white light and took them step-by-step through feeling the light oozing its way down through their bodies. We breathed it down through every organ, every muscle and every cell. Finally, they both seemed completely relaxed. Ahhhh.

At this point I asked Darlene if she wanted to take a little journey and see what it was like to create a beautiful place where she could imagine herself being surrounded by her loved ones. She said yes. I brought her through the process of seeing herself in a comfortable, safe place... a place where she loved to be. She knew exactly where she wanted to be. She wanted to be in her own bed at her home.

I had never had anyone want to go home to their own bedroom while journeying. What a beautiful thing that she had created such a warm, safe place for herself, that in a moment of being asked to journey anywhere in the universe... she didn't need oceans or mountain views, gardens or castles. She preferred her own bedroom in her own home.

So we continued on, with her in her bedroom, imaging anything else she wanted to have in the room — flowers, pets, favorite items, etc. And then as I explained the process to envision her son and daughter-in-law sitting beside her she suddenly got angry and said, "I don't want to do this anymore!"

I was shocked. What happened?

Darlene became more agitated and my friend broke from her relaxed state. We decided we should stop. My friend thought perhaps Darlene needed more morphine, but my experience up until then was that usually the Reiki was so relaxing that people drifted off to sleep or remained pain-free until the session was over. And her morphine injections hadn't been more than a half hour ago. This agitated state was different from anything I had experienced before with a client. I realized it would be best to leave.

What I found out later, was that Darlene had not wanted to go into the nursing facility. She wanted nothing more than to stay in her own home, and apparently once we started journeying and she was "home" in her mind, it gave her the strength to insist on going home... to her own house and her own bedroom. Her insistence was so complete, that within a day or two, her family brought her back there.

We are taught not to question the results of Reiki... after all, the effects of channeling healing energy and making a spiritual connection are between the person and their own higher power and healing abilities. We don't direct or decide what should happen. And apparently, the way spirit worked in this case, Reiki gave Darlene her voice! She wanted to go home... she didn't want to *imagine* being in her bed with her loved ones around her, she wanted to *be* in her bed with her loved ones around her.

Darlene got her wish. Four days after our Reiki session, she died in her own bed, at home.

> *"There's a world where I can go*
> *And tell my secrets to*
> *...In this world I lock out*
> *all my worries and my fears*
> *In my room, in my room"*

In My Room, lyrics by Eric Martin,
Gary Usher, Brian Wilson, Michelle Gayle

13

Gabriel, Child of Light

In the summer of 2006, my hardest yet most profound lesson began. This was the experience that would open me up, break my heart, fill me with love and inspire me to make changes in my life. It held moments of great joy and deep sadness, and brought forth the gifts of friendship, hope, support and surrender. This is the story of a very special child.

As I thought about writing this book, I wondered if this story should be included. All the other chapters were about experiences I entered into *knowing* that the person I was going to work with already knew that they were going to die soon and they were looking for some comfort. This was different. This was not a hospice call or a family asking me for a spiritual treatment. This was not a sick relative. This was a family looking for a Reiki treatment for their child.

As I look back at my first visit now, I realize that entering the hospital room in "healer" mode, as opposed to "hospice" mode, might have made all the difference in the experience that was to come. But first, let me go back to the beginning.

One autumn, I had wonderful group of Russian students that came to learn several levels of Reiki with me. They were all friends, and I remember the classes being so joyful and upbeat, and especially interesting when translations were needed or cultural differences made for some humorous situations. These students always brought some delicious treats to class… mmm, how I looked forward to their coming! Since they took the classes that met once a week for four weeks, that meant that by level II Reiki, we had spent eight evenings together over several months.

I usually stayed in touch with my students after classes were finished, and students often called or emailed questions, announcements or just to say hi. I think it was about six months or so after their class, that one of the women called and told me that she had a very dear friend whose grandson had a brain tumor. She wanted to start visiting little Gabriel and doing Reiki for him, and wanted some suggestions on what to do. Even though she was a busy professional, she began stopping by to see him as often as she could.

Some weeks went by, and one day she called me, asking if I would go visit Gabriel, as he was in the hospital undergoing chemotherapy. I said I would, and called the parents to set up a time.

I'll never forget the moment I walked into that room. For some reason I thought Gabriel would be a toddler! In my mind, he would be sitting up, perhaps surrounded by toys and playthings. I think that somehow in my own being I couldn't fathom the idea of a four-month-old baby getting chemo for a brain tumor, so in my mind I was picturing a four-year-old. But there he was, the sweetest, tiniest little thing, nestled up against his mother, breastfeeding. His eyes were closed, his little hand curled up. A bandage. A tube. A hospital bracelet. His mother, Karoliina, was so beautiful lying there with her long black hair framing her face and her delicate hand lightly holding her son. Although peacefully lying with her baby, Karoliina's face showed worry and exhaustion.

There were other people in the room and I remember introducing myself as I entered, but I only have Gabriel and Karoliina's faces etched in my memory… to this day I remember the love and sweetness illuminating from their bed.

Gabriel's father, Peter, introduced everyone, and then began telling me the medical details of his son's cancer. He mentioned what type of tumor, and where specifically it was located. My mind tried to grasp these big medical words that weren't from my world, and I think I might have heard "two or three months" as part of a diagnosis. I remember thinking how hard this must be for this handsome young father to be dealing with. I had no words at this point and didn't even want to have Peter continue explaining the details that were so serious and scary and painful for him to say. And yet they were looking to *me* to say something… do something. And so I decided to change the energy.

I smiled. I moved slowly. I remember saying something about not needing to know all the medical specifics, that instead I wanted to focus on bringing some peace and calm into the room. I decided to start by introducing a new "smell" into the room. I asked them if that would be ok. I took out a bottle of essential oil, placed a few drops in my palms and asked the others if they wanted a drop as well. They did. Then I asked if it was ok to sit on the bed. I remember slowly waving my hands over the baby's face and holding my hands there for a moment so he could experience the aroma. Karoliina breathed it in as well, and I could feel all those in the room relax.

Gently, I laid my hands on the baby and waited for the healing energy to flow. He was so small that my two hands covered from the back of his head, all the way down to the base of his spine, where, we later found out, there was also a small tumor.

I don't remember much else. In that hour I quietly let the healing energy flow from my hands into this little being while the other's watched. Somehow, I felt a great confidence. I trusted what I had learned and allowed the healing energy to flow through me and out through my hands. I used the Reiki symbols that project love, emotional healing and even karmic healing. Besides the physical comfort, I felt guided to work towards his spiritual healing as well. I felt both honored and humbled to be able to work on this sweet baby. And I really respected the fact that his family was doing everything they could for this child, including complementary therapies.

It wasn't until after I left the hospital and was back in my car that I remember having feelings of sadness, inadequacy and disbelief. How can little babies come into this world with cancer? How can I help his parents handle the worry? Was it right to stay light and positive when I barely understood the situation? It was heartbreaking to see tubes of chemicals flowing into little Gabriel, yet heartwarming to see how he gazed at his mother's face and comforted himself at her breast.

When that first treatment had finished, Peter asked if I could come to their home the next week… the chemo would be over by then and Gabriel would be back home. I said I would be happy to. And so another journey was about to begin… a journey that continues to this day.

A week later, my home visits with Gabriel began. Gabriel's crib was right next to his parents' bed, but most times he was in their bed next to his mother. Sometimes I would sit next to Gabriel and his mother as he slept or nursed. And sometimes I got to hold Gabriel in my arms as I sent him healing energy, and it was so sweet. However, within a few sessions, I really felt that Gabriel was trying to communicate with me on a higher level. He was only months old, but there was a bigger story. His spirit, his soul, was an old soul. Why was he here? Why did he enter this world with a serious disease? And was there some message he came to tell us that we weren't able to understand?

I decided to ask another Reiki Master who was also a therapist to join me in a couple of my sessions. I asked her because I knew she also had some psychic abilities and could perhaps communicate with Gabriel on a different level. I also felt that the family could use some nutritional counseling so I asked my Reiki teacher who knew more than I about herbs and homeopathy, to begin to work with us. Additionally, I asked the parents if it would be ok to send out an email to every energy healer I knew, asking people if they had time to stop by the house and spend some time doing Reiki on Gabriel. And if they couldn't stop by in person, would they send distant healing energy to little Gabriel, when they could.

I was now experiencing a beautiful circle of caring and giving energy healers, coming together to help the little family through a difficult time. Two of my teachers showed up to give Gabriel treatments and several of my students came too. One woman had a little baby about the same age as Gabriel so we brought him along, and sent healing energy to Gabriel as he lay on the blanket and played with his new little friend. I also found out, that the student who had originally introduced me to the family was coming to see the baby several days a week after work. So Gabriel was receiving Reiki, practically on a daily basis. And he began to thrive.

And then another wonderful thing happened. Gabriel's parents and his two grandparents, who lived nearby, all decided to learn how to do Reiki themselves. They could see the benefits, of course for Gabriel, but also for the stress relief and healing for each other. We'd gather in the grandparent's home and hold a small class to go over the basics of Reiki, practice the healing techniques, meditate, eat, and laugh. Sometimes Karoliina would hold Gabriel during the class, other times he slept. And it was so beautiful to see this whole family come together, using their healing touch, positive intention and love to create a healing environment for themselves and their little baby.

I was learning many lessons about being a compassionate healer while becoming a more highly skilled practitioner. I was also learning how to create a healing community. Reiki was not all that well known at this time, and I saw how important it was to start connecting the different Reiki and energy healers in the area. I was learning how comforting it is for people to know that they are surrounded by other caring people in the community during difficult times.

A month after meeting Gabriel, Karoliina and Peter, I sent out this email:

> *I am requesting that you send Reiki healing energy and your personal prayers to a very special little being. His name is Gabriel. He is only five months old and is battling cancerous tumors in his spine and brain. I believe the "reasons" that this beautiful spirit has come to earth with such a condition is being spiritually addressed and cared for in an amazing way by his parents, grandparents and family friends. Reiki has become a daily ritual for this family, so I'm asking you all to send healing to support the entire family. Additionally, he will resume chemotherapy next week, so sending Reiki to support his little system and to his mother who is nourishing him will be helpful. I am happy to keep you updated as we work through this as a healing community.*

The response was overwhelming. The email was passed around and I began receiving messages of support, more offers to help, and emails from other energy workers with suggestions and advice to aid in Gabriel's recovery. Throughout the months, Gabriel grew stronger. His family was trying to balance western medicine with other holistic and complimentary therapies. It wasn't easy. Each round of chemotherapy or radiation produced new worries and setbacks. He hadn't been given a clean bill of health, but Gabriel did experience his first Christmas. The family was experiencing some degree of normalcy, and the network of healers and friends had grown. By springtime it appeared there was no new cancer growth. I joyfully put out this email:

Dear Friends,

I realized that it has been quite some time since I gave you news about my favorite little Reiki Baby. It seems like ages ago that I first stepped into his hospital room, and looked at the frail little guy, only 4 months old, with his little chemotherapy tube attached to one side, and his beautiful mother lying in the bed next to him.

It has been quite a journey, but the light and love that you all have sent, along with the countless energy treatments given to him in person by friends and volunteers has helped him and his entire family to stay strong thru this ordeal. At different intervals I have suggested healers of different modalities, so he is being supported in many different ways. We even had Gabriel out to my Reiki Master's farm, where he and other healers worked in new and different ways to understand and shift the energy towards healing ... I think even the horses were working on him!!! My teacher sees him now every other week, and it has become a beautiful healing, learning and friendship experience for all of us.

All during this time he continued his chemo (and some radiation). I won't get into specifics other than he looks very good, and is getting strong. He is now growing hair, laughs and giggles all the time, and the intensity of HIS energy guides and teaches us as well. He is now starting some new procedures at Children's Memorial – and our prayers are that this will be the final step towards complete recovery. Please continue sending your healing to him, his doctors and nurses as well.

Gabriel turned a year old last month, and the celebration was heartwarming and joyous. I know his family shares in my gratitude to all of YOU.

For a year, this baby and his family were the central focus of my life. As I learned new lessons and techniques, I grew as a practitioner and teacher, but also as a person. And I was very aware that Gabriel had become my teacher. He awakened myself and others to the subtleties of energy healing, directed us in working with him, and communicated his messages to us in ways I had never experienced before. If you've ever walked into a place that made you feel uplifted, like the mountains, or at the seashore, in a temple or church, you know what it felt like when I entered a room where Gabriel was. It was light and sweet and peaceful. He carried a very special energy with him. And if part of his reason for being here on earth was to gather a bunch of strangers together to become family, he had certainly accomplished that! This was such an amazing journey, with ups and downs, concerns and delights. A journey that kept moving forward positively... until one day in early summer.

I remember entering the apartment and it felt totally different. Gabriel could barely lift his little head from his mother's shoulder and I remember asking her what was happening. She thought perhaps he had the flu. I hoped she was right, but I knew it was not just physical. There was a shift. His energy was off... it wasn't sparkling and light. It was heavy and tired and hard for me to read.

Within a few days, Gabriel was growing weaker and so we decided to bring him out to my Reiki teacher's horse farm. As I look back now, this was the beginning of our preparation for his death. We wanted Gabriel surrounded by blue skies, clean air and the people who loved him. We would all lay with him on a blanket in the grass with the sound of birds singing and the whinnying of horses nearby. We took turns doing energy work. We allowed Karoliina and Peter to have time strolling through nature with their son, or taking a nap, or receiving support in any way they needed. We provided new memories out in nature that would hopefully be recalled more often than memories in hospital rooms.

And of course, we prayed for a miracle. Just as my hospice patient, Charlie's family had asked for the miracle. But as we learned, sometimes the miracle is not in changing the way things are, but in changing the way we accept, embrace and cherish the experience. We find the joy and the grace in the lessons that are given to us.

Gabriel had already performed his miracles, and now he was getting ready to leave this world. I could feel it in my soul, but I wondered why. Why now? Some things are beyond our understanding. So I prayed for strength and guidance as my focus shifted from physical healing to embracing Gabriel's journey into death. My requests for healing from my healing community were now for support, understanding and comfort for the family. It was also to surround Gabriel in light and love in preparation for his journey back to spirit.

Shortly after returning from the farm, Gabriel was admitted to the pediatric ICU. Once again, Karoliina lay with her baby on a small hospital bed. She and Peter spent the long summer days living round-the-clock in the little hospital room, cherishing every moment they had with their son. Grandparents, other family members, close friends and healers were all graciously welcomed to share in Gabriel's last days. We were grateful for the support and pain relief offered by western medicine, while we continued to gather in the energy of the healing light, as we had done so many times before. Often times there were seven or eight of us squished in his little room. We would all hold hands and do a meditation to bring in the light, envisioning it entering every one of us, acknowledging the healing and love that Gabriel brought to us, and asking the universal life force energy to heal the physical, emotional and spiritual bodies of all who were there. And we affirmed what a beautiful, although painful, journey this had been.

I never suggested journeying with Gabriel and his family. They were all so intuitively connected that it wasn't even necessary. And we had all experienced Gabriel "communicating" with us so clearly, that we knew it would always continue. And so eventually, my visits again became a time of few words, a time of raising the energy to bring some joy and lightness to a hospital room. We used the oils. Sometimes we meditated or prayed. We did Reiki. But my greatest joy at this time, and what I remember most, was just holding Gabriel's little hand.

When Gabriel left us in the physical realm, it brought forth all the questions and pain that arise when a life is so short. And it made me deeply question my healing work, as well. I then realized that part of embracing death's journey is to ponder the lessons learned, acknowledge the huge loving family Gabriel created, and honor his life, no matter how brief. I knew I needed to write a final email to our healing community. And so despite my deep sadness I opened myself up to feel Gabriel's presence. He reminded me that it is a beautiful gift to know how to be with someone as they journey back into the spirit world. I truly felt his presence as he guided me to write to our healing community once more. I wrote:

> *Our wonderful little Reiki baby, healer and friend, passed away peacefully Wednesday night. I know the Angels sang and warm, loving arms embraced his beautiful soul as he returned to Spirit after such a short, but special life. He was a healer in the truest sense, bringing people together, raising the energy of all who came around him, and always teaching us new lessons. I never would have expected that my most profound lessons of healing, comfort, energy work and hospice would be brought to me by an infant...and the amazing group of healers who came together in his behalf.*
>
> *Gabriel's parents, Peter and Karoliina, were at his side every moment of eastern and western healing therapies, with love and patience. They never abandon their search for healing, yet gracefully accepted Gabriel's final decision that he was ready to go. Our support and healing of the family will continue as we share in their sadness.*
>
> *I am so grateful that so many of you held Gabriel in your healing thoughts and in your hearts for so long. His family was so appreciative of the many visits, healing circles and*

emails from the Reiki community. I know Gabriel will remain in our hearts and connected in Spirit forever.

Look up tonight…there's a new star in the heavens!!!

I had a class scheduled to go to New Mexico within two weeks of Gabriel's death. I sometimes wonder if the timing of that was divinely guided because Karoliina decided to come with me. What was planned as a teaching trip also became a time of healing and reflecting for his mother and me. And, most importantly, it was a time of connecting with my dear little teacher and friend.

"Oh very young what will you leave us this time?
You're only dancing on this earth for a short while"
…And though you want to last forever
you know you never will…
And the goodbye makes the journey harder still"

Oh Very Young, lyrics by Cat Stevens

14

The Journey into My Heart

The time I had spent with Gabriel, his family, and my spiritual community had moved me into a new place in my life. I was dedicated to making Reiki and energy healing my life's work, and also very drawn to the healing energies of New Mexico. Our children were in college and my husband and I were now considering how to move into new phases of our lives. I was aware that circumstances of my life were changing rapidly, some of them beyond my control. Situations that had been my grounding and security, including my home and marriage, were suddenly unstable. The country was experiencing huge changes in finances, politics, global awareness and technological changes. Since 9/11 our country had become very fear-based and most of the clients now coming to me were facing issues of job loss, money issues and stress-related health issues. Many people were questioning their life purpose.

I had lived my entire life in the Chicago area, and now longed for the mountains, open air, blues skies and new opportunities to expand and grow. I needed to connect even more with the spiritual energies that were so easy for me to feel up on the mesa or high in the mountains. Although my husband and I had travelled to New Mexico so many times together, and had planned to move there to start a new life, it was becoming clear to me that his life was going in a different direction. We wouldn't be moving to New Mexico together.

So finally, after another year of soul searching, I got in my car with my dog, Buster, and under an August full moon I set out to start a new journey in New Mexico. For three days my dog and I discovered new territory, stopping to explore little towns, river walks and southern cooking.

After a short period of moving around in Santa Fe, I found myself living about ten miles out of town, in a lovely little apartment. I had never lived with so much open space around me or seen so many brilliant stars. I started waking every morning early enough to walk Buster while watching spectacular sunrises over the mountains. And I fell asleep to a quiet unknown in the big cities... with only the sound of howling coyotes to break the silence.

I also immersed myself in the art and culture of Santa Fe and northern New Mexico, while making time to take new classes in energy work, art & yoga. I was invigorated and energized to start teaching and practicing Reiki again. And rather than volunteer in hospice or try to target my Reiki practice towards the elderly, I decided to see what spirit had in store.

Most of the new students I taught in Santa Fe were already in some sort of holistic healing modality or were massage therapists. Some had taken energy classes a long time ago and now wanted to get re-introduced to Reiki. And happily, some physicians, nurses and therapists were signing up for classes to expand their understanding of energy healing to compliment their medical specialties. It was a different experience and I was learning a lot from each of my students. I was learning more about how energy work fits into day-to-day life and it seemed that my lessons in using "spiritual Reiki at the end of life" were over, at least for the time being.

And then spirit opened another door of opportunity for me. I met a woman who had written a book about dying. She had been a hospice nurse for over forty years, and realized that people needed to accept death as another phase of life, and understand exactly what happens during the months, days and hours preceding death. Since I thought I might resume my hospice work in Santa Fe at some point, I thought I should take her class to get some new awareness of the death process. What I received in her class was so much more than an education, it was a healing.

One of her many gifts in teaching the class, was to slowly and beautifully take you through a demonstration of what the last breath of life is like. As she explained the changes in the body and the breathing, the room filled with a beautiful, almost sacred energy and despite over twenty-five people in the class, you could hear a pin drop. It was magical and beautiful, and yet as I left the class and walked out into the warm summer night, a wave of sadness and grief came over me.

"Why?" I wondered.

And suddenly I realized that she had bridged the gap with my own father's death. I was with him until an hour before his death, but I hadn't been with him as he left his body. Through Reiki and sending distant healing to my father, I knew the connection was there and sometimes I even felt him around me. But until that moment, I hadn't realized that an important piece was missing – the understanding of how gentle and easy and *freeing* the last breath of life truly is.

For weeks, we discussed, relived, shared and explored the physical circumstances relating to death and dying. It was beautiful, healing and informative. But we didn't talk about connecting energetically. We learned many things about what to say and how to say it. But still, we didn't discuss how to connect non-verbally. So I was anxious to have another opportunity to journey at the time of death, and bring my newfound insights into practice as well. I began to write about the process. I began to ask other practitioners if they were facilitating journeying the same way I was.

And then the next lesson presented itself. This was again going to be a hard lesson, but one that would teach me about journeying in a very new and different way. I became aware that my dog was starting on his final journey, too.

Buster had been my constant companion of fourteen years. He had always been so energetic and had an enthusiastic puppy approach to life. He was with me as I started on my journey to become an energy worker, lying under the Reiki table for almost every client I ever had and he especially enjoyed picking one student to sit next to as I taught classes in my home.

One time, after all the students had left class, Buster continued to sit in the place where I would do the Reiki attunements. He was always good at letting me know what he wanted. He wanted me to attune him to the Reiki energy, too. So I did my first dog attunement!

Once in New Mexico, Buster took on the role of my protector. It wasn't always easy for him when I moved several times to new living arrangements, but he seemed to feel secure in the little bed I had in the back of my car. Together we learned to climb mountains and hike long distances. He was extremely proud of himself when I would get lost on trails and he'd put me back on the right path. He loved the dog parks and would run and play with his new friends, and whine and whimper if we passed the parks and I didn't stop the car to let him out.

I remember the first time I took Buster on the mesa at Ojo Caliente. The climb is quite steep for about five minutes, before flattening out on top of the mesa. He was already 12 years old and I wondered if it would be a difficult climb for him. Silly me... I'd forgotten that with four legs climbing was pretty easy. He had no problem and loved exploring the mesa. We went up there together many times. But as he approached fourteen, Buster's back legs were getting stiff, and his hips weak, and he just didn't run much anymore. He had stopped jumping up on the bed and now slept on the floor. He sometimes hesitated as he jumped up into the car, and we had worked out a routine for keeping my hands behind his butt and giving a little push if didn't have enough "oomph" to get into the car.

So on one particular day when we were heading up the mesa, I decided to stay behind Buster so I could support his rear end if he tired or came upon some rocks that were a little too steep for him. It was working well... he'd walk along and every now and then when he'd hesitate I'd give a little push. We were just about at the top, when I saw that he was breathing pretty heavily, so I sat on a rock and I told him to sit, so we could rest. He sat for just a moment, then got up and looked me in the eye, and I swear I could hear the dog say "sorry, but I'm done climbing... I'm outta here!" And he headed straight down the steep trail as quickly as he could!

It wasn't as frightening as the night my father fainted at dinner, but the message was just as clear. I was once again starting on an end-of-life journey... this time with my dog. I knew we still had lots of time together, but I also knew that Reiki was going to be a big part of our final journey. For most of us, our pets truly are a blessed part of the family and the reality of losing a pet that loves you unconditionally is very difficult.

Our hikes remained on flatter ground after that. I noticed him sleeping a lot more and his appetite was changing. His once strong body got weaker and his excitement for exploring new places lessened. But not surprisingly, his determination at begging for people food never seemed to wane! I needed to really be aware of his needs and to start a new connection process with my little friend.

I've never been a pet communicator. I had studied it a bit and sometimes practiced visualizing messages to my dog knowing that they communicate by seeing our mental pictures. The thought had crossed my mind to try "journeying" with Buster, but I hadn't yet taken the time to do so.

But spirit again had other plans. A huge lesson came one day when I had gone for an energy treatment for myself. Buster had been in the car with me, but it was too hot to leave him inside the car for an hour or so. As I approached the other practitioner's office I called and asked if there was some place that I could tie up Buster in the shade, outside the office. When we arrived, there was a bowl of water waiting for us in a nice, shady spot right by the front door.

Usually, when I left Buster outside a store, a restaurant or someone's house (as we often do in Santa Fe, which is an extremely dog-friendly city,) he just lays down and waits for me. But this time, he barked.

"He'll stop in a minute," I said. "Once he knows I'm not coming right back out, he'll settle down."

We started the treatment. Soft music was playing, and I felt the energy worker's hands gently touching the bottom of my feet as I relaxed on the table. All was calm… except for Buster who wouldn't stop barking. It wasn't like him to not settle down. I knew he liked to be with me when I'd get a treatment, but I thought he'd "give it up" after a few minutes. He didn't. Hmmm, what was I going to do?

I could already feel a spiritual energy around me, so I focused on connecting with Buster and communicating with him that everything was ok. And then I did the oddest thing. I visualized Buster floating into the room and lying down right on my chest. I visualized putting my arms around him and imagined him floating right down into my own heart. It was kind of like putting a baby into one of those little snuggly sacks that mothers wear to hold their babies close. But there was no snuggly. I watched Buster's body melt right into my heart center, and only his head was left sticking out.

What a strange thought. Where had that come from? And yet I found myself imagining my arms around him and telling him it was ok. I had brought my dog into my heart in an effort to calm him down. I was journeying with Buster. Just as I realized that he was no longer barking, the other practitioner said, "I can feel what you're doing with Buster... that's really cool how you two are so connected."

It was more than cool... it was the simple visualization that I realized would work with our pets. We don't need to create a *place* to journey to with our pets. We *ARE* the place that our pets most want to be. With us. Within our hearts. One with their loving owners.

My own treatment continued and I stopped thinking about Buster until suddenly I realized he had been quiet for quite some time. And then I got a little nervous. What if this was happening because it was his time to die, and within the spiritual energy of a healing treatment Buster had left his body and come to be with me to say goodbye. On one hand, what a beautiful thing that would be, but on the other,

I wasn't ready for my faithful friend and companion to leave so suddenly.

I thought to myself, "Buster if you're ok, please bark again." And I visualized him on the porch, waking up from his nap and looking around to remember where he was.

"Arrf." He barked. And a moment later he barked again, and I smiled and knew he was still with us.

I realized then that there is a way to journey with our animals. I was once again amazed that these little, easy processes were coming to me that provide so much comfort and peace. I now knew that I had a way to connect with my dog now and forever. And I began to practice bringing my pet into my heart energy in a very real and ritualistic way.

Eventually, Buster got very lethargic. He was sick. So even though I knew that I would not do any drastic life-saving procedures on a 14 year-old dog, I brought him to the vet for blood work and an ultrasound to see if any of the fatty tumors on the outside were actually cancer tumors on the inside. And I was correct. His spleen had a large tumor and the cancer had spread to his liver. It broke my heart.

The time in the vet's office was stressful, so I brought Buster to a park and we lay in the grass for a long time. I meditated and prayed for guidance. Was it time to put him down? I decided it was not.

It's a wonderful thing that we are able to put our animals out of their pain and misery. But I've also learned a lot about the stages of dying and understood that the later stages of little food and lots of sleep are also an important part of making the transition and leaving the physical body. What often looks like pain or agitation is the spirit releasing from the body to connect with the spiritual world, and then coming back into the body and regaining consciousness. What seems to us to be discomfort can be the *labor pains* of dying, so to speak. Yes, he was dying, but even though I could have put him out of his discomfort, he had stages to go through to be ready for death. Buster would sometimes lift his head and bark, or moan, or move his head back and forth as if *listening* to someone or something else. I do believe spirits were visiting him, preparing him and comforting him. I realized that although painful for me to witness, he *needed* this time of preparation to leave his body and to be ready to let go of me. So I continued to comfort him as best I could and would "bring him into my heart" as I did Reiki treatments on him.

Eventually his physical body had deteriorated to a point that I had to consider putting him down. Just like every other pet owner who faces this time in their animal's life, I began to pray that he would die. I had given him permission to go. I thanked him, I told him he had been a wonderful companion and enriched my life enormously. I explained that I would see him again, that we'll stay connected. And yet, he didn't die.

And so the lesson of caring for a life enough to help end it was now at hand. Of course, I could have waited until he died naturally, but he was now in pain. I also believe that dogs that have dedicated their lives to being a companion *will* themselves to hang on for their masters. My other choice was that I could create a deliberate, beautiful and spiritual setting for my dog and me to be together — connected as he moved into the non-physical world. This became my choice.

I picked a spot under a tree where we sat together for over an hour before the vet arrived to help the process of comfortably, peacefully letting go. I created mental pictures of memories together for him to "see." I fed him some treats... a little steak, some eggs and even some chocolate. And finally I journeyed with him. I brought him into my heart. And I felt him resting there… being at peace in my heart energy. And when the vet arrived, I held and comforted my little guy until he was free.

~ ~

I regularly practice connecting with him, visualizing him coming into my heart. Several times he has come to me in my dreams. I used to bring him into my heart because *he* needed it, and now I bring him there because *I* need to feel him. And sometimes when he must know that I need to connect, I hear him bark.

> *"I've changed my ways a little: I cannot now*
> *Run with you in the evening along the shore,*
> *Except in a kind of dream;*
> *and you, if you dream a moment,*
> *You see me there."*

Robinson Jeffers

15

No Longer Afraid to Say Good-bye

As I looked back over the years, I could see how I moved from the misunderstanding and the fear of death, into the realm of acceptance that death is a natural process of both the spiritual and the physical. I understood that death is an energy taking us from one place to the next… a natural flow. It's not an ending, it's a transformation. Finally I could accept, embrace and actively be a supportive part of the end-of-life journey. More importantly I was no longer afraid to say good-bye. Death had become another stage of life… the final stage; one which holds enormous amounts of sharing, healing and love. And I understood that even when it is a sudden death, the spiritual connection could be felt and cherished.

I also realized that since we can't ever know exactly when someone is going to die, perhaps it's never too early to practice connecting spiritually to those friends and family that we don't get to see very often.

With that in mind, on a trip back to Chicago, I visited an elderly relative whose health was failing. I didn't know if I'd get a chance to see her again. We sat together outside the front door of her apartment, looking out at the tall plants, waterfall and flowers that decorated the rainforest-like lobby of her retirement community. As I held her hand for comfort, we talked a little, and then I asked her if she'd like me to do a little energy work on her. This would not be the first time — I had treated her before in the past. She smiled, nodded yes and then closed her eyes. I continued to hold her hand, but I used my other hand to flow Reiki into her heart center. We both began to feel the gentle flow of energy.

Suddenly I saw a hawk swoop down over the atrium window. It felt magical and spiritual, and I quickly asked, "Did you see that?"

And as my dear friend, tired and frail, now into her nineties, opened her eyes and looked up, the hawk appeared and swooped down over us again. I knew it was a special moment, and I also knew it was the time to journey.

So once again, I closed my eyes and began speaking slowly and lovingly, again practicing what I had done many times before. I realized how comfortable this now was for me. The words came easily as I asked her to imagine she was in a safe, comfortable and loving place surrounded by her loved ones... a place to share thoughts and memories with all the people she loved and wished to see.

"Right here," she replied. "I love sitting right here."

As I sat and held her hand and sent love and healing energy into her heart, I communicated with her non-verbally. I told her everything I had wanted to say, and pictured us sitting, talking and enjoying our company together as we had done so many times before. A little while later, after having fallen asleep for just a few minutes, she opened her eyes and looked at me. It was more than a casual glance, it was an acknowledgment of our connection, and she smiled at me.

"Will you do me a favor?" I asked. "Once I go back to Santa Fe, will you, every now and then, try to imagine me sitting here with you, holding your hand?"

She smiled and nodded. I told her that anytime she felt like she needed some "good energy" or just wanted to visit with me, all she had to do is imagine being out there on the foyer, and I'd join her there. I told her we could do that forever. I was so grateful that it felt so easy to tell her I loved her. I let her know that I would always be there to visit with her. She just had to use her imagination. I believe she understood.

Now, many months later, she is still with us. When she is feeling well, we talk on the phone. But other times, she tells me, she goes into her imagination and remembers me sitting holding her hand. I believe these are the times that I suddenly think of her, and so I stop what I'm doing to feel the connection with her. Sitting in the dryness of New Mexico, I often go to the rainforest outside her apartment, hold her hand, send her energy and together we enjoy the peace, love and final days of her journey.

I have learned that the time we spend with people as they enter into their deaths is truly a blessing if you approach it that way.

I believe everyone can learn to embrace the journey into death. Be with your loved ones, your friends, your hospice patients and your animals, ready to receive lessons and experience new levels of togetherness, peace and joy. Spend time during your visits practicing journeying, meditating or connecting energetically. As you lightly touch their hands, silently send love, forgiveness, acceptance and peace to their hearts. Know that in those moments at their bedside, spirit will guide you, as I was guided. Laugh together, cry together, share stories, poems or music, and speak what's in your hearts. Embrace the opportunity to be with another as they leave the physical world, and behold the miracle. Just as we rejoice in the miracle of birth, rejoice in the miracle of death and embrace every moment. Embracing the end–of–life journey is an eternal gift… for both of you.

"Now it begins,
Now it starts
Even death can't part us now"

One Hand One Heart, *lyrics by Stephen Sondheim*

Acknowledgements

I am deeply grateful to all the beautiful souls who allowed me to be with them during their end-of-life journeys. As I wrote this book, I felt their guidance, lessons and support. And I am just as grateful to their family members who supported my work, encouraged me to write about these experiences and shared their memories and opinions with me.

I am equally grateful to the people who have inspired and guided me on this journey by writing their own books, lecturing and being bold enough to talk about the difficult subject of death. The first was Dr. Brian Weiss, whose fascinating and courageous book "Many Lives Many Masters" opened my awareness to the spiritual nature of death. My attendance at his seminar nearly twenty-five years ago was a turning point in my spiritual journey.

As I began writing this book, I was very aware of music coming to me as I wrote each chapter, and I honor and thank every lyricist in this book for their sweet words that have become another way of illustrating the peace, miracles, love and sadness we all experience and share through music.

I was blessed to find Michael Soto for my Reiki Master teacher and lifelong friend. He carefully took me through the lessons of learning to work with energy and how to be a compassionate healer. And to my other teachers and the Reiki community, too numerous to name, I am also indebted. I have so much gratitude for the many Reiki students who listened to my stories and experiences—often bringing me to new levels of awareness. They too, have been my teachers.

A big thank you to Denys Cope author of "Death: A Natural Passage" whose seminar inspired me to tell my story, and who encouraged me throughout the writing process of this book. And a heartfelt thank you to Jennifer Moore who provided a peaceful place for me to retreat and write, and then offered her excellent editing skills and supportive advice.

But my deepest feelings of gratitude go to my father, who set me on this path, to my amazing pet, Buster who brought the lesson into a larger realm by being sure I included animals in the journeying process, to Kristina, Michael and Sebastien, whose courage inspired and taught me more than they will ever know, to my dear Sarah who always keeps my heart filled with love and joy, and to Roger who filled my life and my heart with encouragement, love and new puppies during the writing of this book.

For More Information

Wendy Jordan is a teacher of all levels of Usui Reiki and teaches the process of "Reiki Journeying" as part of her Reiki Master Classes. "End-of-Life Reiki Journeying" is also offered as separate class.

She is also available for training or seminars for hospice workers, nursing groups or any other "healing" groups that would like specific information on spiritual healing or journeying.

For people currently embracing the end-of-life journey with a loved one, private sessions are available by appointment, and include individual Reiki sessions for the person preparing for death, individual family members and group journeying sessions.

Reiki sessions are available in person in Santa Fe, or by distance healing via the internet and phone.

Wendy can be reached at:

JoyousJournies.com
Reikijournies@gmail.com
or on Facebook at
Wendy Jordan Healing Arts

Thank you for opening your hearts to being present, compassionate and supportive of the end-of-life journey. Many Blessings.

CPSIA information can be obtained at www.ICGtesting.com
Printed in the USA
LVOW06s0532060115

421611LV00001B/43/P

9 781452 593067